FULL
WATTAGE!

*A Practical Guide to Living
an Engaging and Purposeful Life
Worth Celebrating*

LIZ FLETCHER BROWN

PAISLEY PRINT PUBLISHING
Davidsonville, MD

First edition published 2013

ISBN-13: 978-0-9855694-5-7

Library of Congress Control Number: 2012911600

Printed in U.S.A.

PAISLEY PRINT PUBLISHING
www.PaisleyPrintPublishing.com
PO Box 346, Davidsonville, MD 21035

Dedication

*To all those brilliant ones awaking to the fact that
they came here to do more—to be more.
This is your time to shine. And shine you will.
I can hardly wait...*

Now is your time to live with Full Wattage!

Acknowledgments

Thank you from the bottom of my heart to:

My mum who taught me to always be myself, and to follow my dreams no matter what. I love you mum.

Joann Saraydarian who exemplifies living with Full Wattage more than anyone I know. Joann, you ROC this world!

Shawn Moore, one of the brightest stars in the galaxy, who has always believed in me anytime I dared to doubt myself. Shawn, thank you for being so instrumental in helping me develop this work. I truly couldn't have done it without you.

Diane Davis, who was my constant support and indispensible sounding board throughout this project. Thank you for always being there every time I said, "Could you just take one more look at…"

Nicolette Beard, Lynn Amende and Sonia Feldman for helping me refine the manuscript. Thank you for your keen eyes and open hearts. Your suggestions made this book so much better.

Deb Caruso, Christie Pirrung, Sue Woolsey, Cheryl Miller, Sonia Feldman, Debbie Fortier and Mary Wilson-Byrom for graciously opening their homes and hosting intimate gatherings of friends. The feedback I got at these events as I birthed this work was priceless.

Judith McCabe (for bringing so much light into my world), Hiram Bullock (love you always), and John Hale Davis (for daring me to imagine, and for introducing me to some of the foundational concepts that I leapt off of). It's good to know there are three more angels watching over us.

Dawn Josephson, my editor, who took my words and made them shine, taking this book to a whole new level. And to Peri Poloni-Gabriel who produced the cover from the original artwork and designed the book's beautiful interior. You were both an absolute joy to work with. Thank you for sharing your expertise, your creative genius, and for partnering with me in this exciting process.

They say it takes a village...How true that is. My village also includes—Melanie Wright, Norma Moore, John Collings, Marguerite Pelissier, Bernadette Zorio, Cheryl Corson, Sierra Stearns, Lori Taylor, Sharon Bodé, Jean Berube and Janice Pavillar. Thank you for your ongoing love, support and encouragement.

To my colleagues at the National Speakers Association (especially the DC Chapter) for so generously sharing your wisdom and your guidance.

To all of the workshop participants and clients who have taught me more than I could ever teach them.

To Barbara Marx Hubbard and Marian Head for allowing me to reprint their powerful words from *The Suprasexual Revolution: Towards the Birth of a Universal Humanity* (Marlin Press).

To my sweet JJ (Embers Just Jolli) who was a constant 4-legged companion for 16 years and a bolt of joy and enthusiasm wherever he went. He showed me many pathways to the heart, and I miss him.

And most especially to my greatest love, Francis, who gives me reason to dance with joy every day. Francis, I love you more than words could ever express. Thank you for always being there for me, for holding me up when I fall, and for always cheering me on. My love...we did it! Time to do the Happy Dance!

Contents

Introduction

MRS. JAMIESON'S BALLET CLASS WAS not your average dance class. The studio was housed in an old renovated fire station in Bellingham, Washington, and much of the original structure had been maintained.

On a warm day she would roll back the great big red doors that faced the street, allowing the gawkers and the simply curious a peak into the magical world of ballet.

Many of Mrs. Jamieson's adult students, myself included, had danced professionally at some time in our lives, but had long since hung up our pointe shoes. Nevertheless, we showed up three times a week and put our bodies through the rigors of ballet because of our sheer love of dance.

Other students were adult contemporary dancers who wanted to develop their technique in a way only ballet could provide. And occasionally, some young whippersnapper from the dance department at the local university would take the class—reminding us all of what our bodies could do when we were 20.

One of the things I loved about Mrs. Jamieson was her sense of artistry. Instead of doing our routine barre exercises to yet another nondescript *Piano for Ballet* CD, she carefully chose variations of the classics that would bring out the qualities she saw in each dancer.

And just when you thought your leg could not lift into one more grand battement, she would energize us with stories from her professional career and of the great dancers she had partnered with. Occasionally she would entertain us all by vividly describing her wacky dream from the night before and somehow magically make it relevant to the next plié or pirouette.

But what I admired most about Mrs. Jamieson was her unabashed love of dance and her contagious enthusiasm that touched everyone who walked through the studio door. Her very presence radiated a powerful sense that anything was possible.

I learned a lot from Mrs. Jamieson—and not just about ballet. Looking back on her classes now, what stands out the most is when she would say, "Ladies, I don't care how high you lift your leg or how many pirouettes you do. What I do care about is that you dance with *Full Wattage!*"

And dance with Full Wattage we did! We were radiant, confident, purposeful, present, joyful, and vitally alive with the power of enthusiasm—not superficial enthusiasm, but deep inner enthusiasm that radiated from the very core of our being. It was the type of enthusiasm that made us feel unstoppable as we fully expressed our unique brilliance to the world.

If only I could live my life the way I danced in Mrs. Jameson's ballet class…

But then again, why not?

So that began my exploration into what it would take to lead an engaging, purposeful life, and in particular into the nature of enthusiasm—how we get it, how we lose it, how we keep it, and how we spread it. And along the way I began to see the connection between enthusiasm, personal power, and brilliance.

The Dance of Business and Life

Leaders from all walks of life cite enthusiasm as one of the most important qualities a person must have. Here are a few of my favorite quotes that exemplify this point:

- Vince Lombardi, the great football coach said, "If you aren't fired with enthusiasm, you will be fired with enthusiasm."
- Businesswoman Mary Kay Ash believed, "A mediocre idea that generates enthusiasm will go further than a great idea that inspires no one."
- Industrialist Henry Ford stated, "Enthusiasm is the yeast that makes your hopes shine to the stars...the irresistible surge of will and energy to execute your ideas."
- And bestselling author and sales expert Og Mandino described the importance of enthusiasm this way: "Every memorable act in the history of the world is a triumph of enthusiasm. Nothing great was ever achieved without it because it gives any challenge or any occupation, no matter how frightening or difficult, a new meaning. Without enthusiasm you are doomed to a life of mediocrity, but with it you can accomplish miracles."

Often, people think that enthusiasm is something you either naturally have or don't have. Some even believe enthusiasm is dependent on external circumstances. But neither is true.

Enthusiasm is the life force that flows through you, and it is your divine birthright.

In this book I will share with you the secrets to living with more enthusiasm, no matter what your situation is. You will discover how to tap into your personal power and brilliance so you can rejuvenate your life, both at work and at home. And you will discover how to create an engaging and purposeful life worth celebrating.

How can a dancer do this? Because dance is about so much more than simply moving your body in a certain way. The world of dance teaches so many lessons, including:

- The importance of following your dreams.
- The value of persistence.
- Why personal discipline is the key to success.
- How not to take rejection personally.
- The skill of working with a team.
- How to deal with prima donnas (literally).
- How to know when to take the stage as the star and when to be a supportive follower.

Over the years, I've learned that we each have something unique to share with the world. And when you share your gifts, you become more vibrant, dynamic, and enthusiastic in all areas of your life. That's why I've spent the past two decades helping individuals re-discover and connect to their Core Brilliance so they (and their organizations) go from ordinary to extraordinary.

So perhaps you are striving to be a more skillful leader, whether it be a leader of your family, your co-workers, your employees, or even yourself! Maybe you are yearning for a deeper sense of purpose and satisfaction in life. Or perhaps you want to feel more self-confident and less overwhelmed and stressed.

You might be tired of "going through the motions," feeling bored and half-awake at best, and are ready to experience being inspired and vibrantly alive!

If any of these scenarios sound like you, you've come to the right place. Follow along and I'll reveal practical ways of bringing greater purpose to your life. Together, we'll explore new possibilities and help you cultivate the skills and confidence you need to finally go after what you really want.

It's time to live your life with FULL WATTAGE!

Your Life Dance...

*holds the secret to living
with Full Wattage!*

A vocation of destiny is the innate calling,
the code of genius that must be expressed
to fulfill our purpose on earth.

It is that which nature created us to do and be.

Our vocations pulse in us with the fierce power
that drives the green shoots up through
the frozen soil in the spring.

We are driven to grow by the force of creation.

In the secret depths of our hearts,
we have known the desire to do more,
to be more, to fully actualize ourselves.

But for most of us, the time has not been right.
We have not been called forth fully.
We've kept ourselves in limited jobs, doing repetitive tasks,
reproducing ourselves, struggling to survive,
and dying young.

Now, we have entered the second life cycle.
Evolutionary crises and opportunity activate
us en masse to expand our lives
from the immediate concerns of self-maintenance
to the survival and development of the larger community.

We are at the threshold of the greatest release of
human creativity the world has ever known.

BARBARA MARX HUBBARD and MARIAN HEAD

CHAPTER 1

How to Keep Your Balance
When the Floor is Rocking

"The journey between who you once were, and who you are now becoming, is where the dance of life really takes place."

BARBARA DE ANGELIS, Personal Growth Pioneer

I'D LIKE TO TAKE YOU back to one of my first experiences in overcoming adversity and the life-changing lesson it taught me about living with enthusiasm.

When I was in my teens I took a trip across the North Sea on the SS Uganda. If you have ever been to a large shipping port or have seen cruise vacation commercials on TV or online, you're familiar with those huge, towering cruise ships that are like floating cities. Well, the SS Uganda was *not* one of those.

The SS Uganda was originally constructed to accommodate only 300 passengers, but it had been "upgraded" to carry 900 more. These additional passengers, of whom I was one, were typically students taking part in educational programs.

Since they couldn't build the ship outwards to create the dormitory style accommodations for the students, they had to build *up*. As a result, the extra weight on the upper decks made the SS Uganda top heavy and caused the ship to make a slightly peculiar motion that got worse as the waves got bigger.

It was a warm, sunny day in June and we were heading home to Scotland after a spectacular cruise that took us all the way to the North Cape of Norway, which is the northern-most point in mainland Europe. It's also the magical Land of the Midnight Sun—truly one of the most hauntingly beautiful places on earth.

My head was dancing with images of a sun that never sets as we crossed the North Sea. But then something happened that shifted my focus…BIG TIME!

I was leaning against the railing of the top deck, staring out to sea and enjoying being lost in my thoughts when I heard footsteps coming toward me. I turned. It was Rick, the ship's program director, and he was frantically trying to get my attention.

I liked Rick. He was one of the older crew members, ruggedly handsome, and an *amazing* dancer. During the entire cruise he had been encouraging me to "think bigger" about my future as a professional dancer.

"Liz," he excitedly said in his deep Scottish brogue, "I've been looking for you. We need you in the theatre right away!"

Later that night we were scheduled to do a dance performance on the main stage of the cruise ship, and I had a relatively small part. But Rick was about to change all that.

"I've been watching you in rehearsals," he said. "Tonight I want you to dance the lead role. And this is your chance to shine. There'll be two talent scouts in the audience from a national TV show, and they're looking for dancers."

At first I was completely taken aback. I had been learning the lead role, but so had two other dancers, both of whom had a lot more experience than me. I hadn't expected to be chosen. But as I thought about it, excitement welled up inside me.

"Yes," I told Rick as I enthusiastically jumped up and down. "I'll do it!"

While I was excited about the opportunity, as the day wore on I found myself feeling more and more nervous about the responsibility. After all, in this lead role the weight of our dance troupe's success rested on my shoulders. But then again, I *had* prepared for this with years of classes and training. I was ready!

In the late afternoon I went back to my cabin to mentally rehearse for my big moment. Then I made my way to the theatre to begin the process of getting my muscles warmed up and ready for action.

About an hour before the curtain was due to rise, we hit stormy weather. It was fairly gentle at first as the ship started to roll from side to side, but it kept getting worse...a lot worse. By show time, we were in a full blown storm. I thought we would definitely be cancelled. But it's true what they say—"The show must go on!"

Just before the performance was about to begin I stood in the wings wondering how I was going to pull it off. The ship was rocking wildly from side to side. Props and all kinds of theatrical paraphernalia were flying around backstage. I was staggering around just trying to stand still.

I turned to Rick, horrified, and said, "This is crazy! How am I going to keep my balance?"

He just smiled confidently and said, "Liz, breathe…and remember, connect to your core."

As a distraction I decided to peek out through the curtains. To my dismay there were only about twenty people in the entire audience. Seasickness was taking its toll.

And that's when I saw them, sitting dead center in the second row—two stoic looking gentlemen. I knew instantly they were the talent scouts. I quickly closed the curtains and said to myself, "Great! Everyone else got sea sick. Why not them? They're going to see me fall flat on my face."

Then the mental chatter began. First I heard the little voice of reason: "Liz, you can do this. It could have been worse. You didn't get sea sick."

Then my self-doubt surfaced: "Are you crazy? How are you going to keep your balance? You *will* fall flat on your face."

Reason again chimed in: "Liz, remember London? That revolving stage? With the six inch heels you had to dance in and the wig that kept falling over your eyes? This'll be a breeze compared to that."

I argued with myself, "A breeze? This isn't a breeze. Any minute now they'll be dropping the life rafts. Besides, if you haven't noticed, there's nobody out there. They're all back in their rooms throwing up!"

Then Rick's words played through my brain: "Liz, you can do it. Just *b r e a t h e*. Connect to your core. You'll be great. On with the show."

So there I was on center stage, holding my opening position. The curtain was gradually rising. All forty eyes were on me as… the boat lurched dramatically. I immediately lost my balance and almost fell on my butt.

I regained my balance momentarily, just as the music began. All I could think about was not falling over…and the two talent scouts judging every move I made.

Unfortunately, despite my best attempts, I was falling all over the place. I saw my chance at stardom going out the window, or should I say, out the porthole.

But then something happened. I again remembered what Rick said. I took a deep breath. I got centered by connecting to my core. And then…I just danced.

As I moved across the stage I was filled with joy and enthusiasm. I tapped into my personal power and allowed my brilliance to shine. Soon I didn't even notice the ship rocking wildly from side to side. In fact, I even managed to integrate the swaying motion into my routine.

When I was done, I took my bow. The audience was eerily silent. "Is anyone even out there?" I wondered. Then I heard "Bravo!" and two pairs of clapping hands.

I did it! I pulled it off. And I got my big break. But even more important, I learned that no matter what the situation, *we have a lot more control than we think.*

Connect to YOUR Core

When I was struggling to keep my balance, I heard Rick's voice telling me to connect to my core.

In dance, our core muscles are the deep muscles at the center of our body. They include the abdominal and back muscles, as well as those of the pelvic floor and hips. Many of our core muscles can't be seen because they are so deep. But when they are strong, the whole body functions more efficiently.

When the core muscles are engaged, everything else can be fluid and relaxed. You can hold your balance, move with great speed, spin like a top, and leap through the air and land like a cat when you are connected to your core. You are also present in the moment, energized, and alive. This is what it means to be dancing with Full Wattage.

For a dancer, you could say that our core is our powerhouse, our inner strength, and the center from which all our movements and energy radiate. It's our brilliance!

When it comes to daily living, what is your powerhouse? Your core? I believe it is the essence of who you are. It's the part of you that is always steady and calm, no matter how chaotic things may be around you.

Your core is that quiet place deep within where you are fully integrated with your values in every area of your life. It's what makes you feel *alive* with a sense of purpose.

When you connect to your core, you listen to your heart first and your head second, and you allow your authentic *brilliance* to shine. As a result, not only is it easier to keep your balance, but you will also be filled with vitality and enthusiasm, no matter how turbulent life gets.

To help you identify your unique core I have included some exercises for you to do. Take the time to answer them honestly and thoroughly. If you don't want to write in this book, you can download the complimentary companion online guide at www. FullWattage.com/resources.

Let's Begin…Think about a specific time in your life when you felt that inner strength—that you were connected to your core.

____I felt that inner strength most in my life when:

_____

_____

_____

_____

_____

_____

Reflecting on that memory, were you resilient during that time? Did you feel you could weather any storm?

Conversely, think about a time when you felt most disconnected from your core.

____I felt most disconnected from my core when:

_____

_____

_____

_____

_____

If you are like most of us, during that time (or times) you were probably feeling overwhelmed, and were "dancing as fast as you can," without necessarily getting where you wanted to go.

Let's face it…we *are* living in extraordinary and often turbulent times. Just turn on the news or the weather channel briefly for evidence of that.

And the pace of our busy lives gives us less opportunity to unwind and truly relax. It's no wonder we often feel so overwhelmed. Yet to succeed in times like these requires more inner strength, more courage, and certainly more focused determination than ever before.

You will experience these things when you tap into the depth of your core, because **your core is your *true powerhouse*.**

Connect to your core and you will also be more productive, creative, and happier. You will have what it takes to follow your dreams. Along the way you will experience more enthusiasm for life despite your present circumstances.

So what is your core? The key elements are:

1. **Your sense of purpose.** Do you hunger for more satisfaction and fulfillment in your life? A feeling that you are making a difference? A reason for being beyond the mundane activities that fill your days? Most people do. So answer this: Who are you *really* and what have you come here to do? What fills you with passion and gives your life meaning?

2. **Your natural strengths, gifts, and talents.** Have you ever felt that you were standing in the wings of life, waiting for your chance to take center stage and to really shine? But somehow that moment never came. Do you feel you possess more strengths, gifts, and talents than you are currently

using yet you don't know *exactly* what they are? My questions to you are: What were you born to do? What can you do better than anyone else?

3. **Your values.** What's most important to you? What are those one or two things that are absolutely non-negotiable? In many ways your values dictate your attitude toward life. What do you *really* believe in? What matters most?

These three elements combine to create your unique "life dance." They are the things you can organize your life around, especially in today's fast changing world. Why? Because when life is moving and shaking, these three things *will not* change. You can grasp them and hold onto them because they are 100% true about you. They are *essential* to who you are. They are also your greatest source of energy, enthusiasm, and joy.

Don't worry if you don't have clarity on these things right now. Stay with me. As you work through this book the answers will come.

The more you live in alignment with your purpose, strengths, and values, the more fully engaged you will be in life. You will be able to weather any storm, no matter how much the floor is rocking. You will have discovered the secret of how to create a life worth celebrating.

And just like the muscles of your body, these three things (your purpose, strengths, and values) are all connected. When you combine your sense of purpose with your unique strengths and your specific values, you will see that there is *nobody* on this planet *exactly* like you. Someone else may have the same life purpose, or strengths, or values. But nobody will have the exact same combination as you, nor will they express them the same way. That's why your "life dance" is specific to you.

There are things for you to do that nobody else can do as well as you. There are people waiting to hear your message, read your words, feel your touch, be uplifted by your smile, and be encouraged by your story.

You have a unique design that makes you unlike any other. And it emanates from your core. That's why connecting to your core is *the* ultimate secret to success and the pathway to living with Full Wattage.

My Promise to You

As we move forward together, I'm going to help you answer the following questions:

- What specifically would make *your life* more meaningful and purposeful? We will address this in Act One, Uncover the Blueprint for Your Life.
- How can you express more of your unique gifts and natural talents in your personal and professional life? This will be the focus of Act Two, Do What You Love and Do Best.
- How can you build your life around the things that *really* matter *to you?* We will explore this in Act Three, Clarify What Matters Most.
- What can you do when you encounter saboteurs along the way? We will deal with them in Act Four, Living With Full Wattage. In this section I'll also share with you many tools and resources to help you create a life worth celebrating.

Throughout each section I'll also share stories and examples of how you can put all this into practice in your life.

I invite you to use this book and this time as an opportunity to renew, recharge, and revitalize…to deepen your connection to your core and to renew your enthusiasm for life.

Your CORE Brilliance

Here is an easy way to remember CORE:

C = Clarify

It's important to get *really* clear on your sense of purpose; your unique strengths, talents, and gifts; and your values. Throughout this book I will help you clarify them with a series of questions and powerful exercises.

O = Organize

Knowing your purpose, strengths, and values is the first step. The second step is to organize your life around them to give them the time and attention they deserve.

R = Release

Sometimes you have to let go of the things that are holding you back and preventing you from living with Full Wattage.

E = Enthusiasm

If you engage your purpose, strengths, and values in life, and release the things getting in your way, then you will experience more energy, enjoyment, and enthusiasm. Guaranteed!

So, are you ready to connect to your CORE and experience the natural enthusiasm, personal power, and brilliance that is your birthright? Are you ready to live an engaging and purposeful life worth celebrating? Are you ready to live with Full Wattage? Then let us begin by exploring why you might be here on earth, at this particular time.

Uncover the Blueprint
for Your Life

Why are you here on earth,
at this particular time?
What brings you energy,
passion, and joy?

CHAPTER 2

Teetering and Tottering

"All movement can be considered to be a series of falls and recoveries; that is, a deliberate unbalance in order to progress, and a restoration of equilibrium for self protection. The nearer the state of unbalance approaches the dangerous, the more exciting it becomes to watch, and the more pleasurable the recovery. This danger zone, which life tends to avoid as much as possible, is the zone in which the dance largely has its existence."

DORIS HUMPHREY, Choreographer and Dance Pioneer

DO YOU EVER FEEL THAT your work is taking up more and more of your mental, emotional, physical, and spiritual energy? On top of that you may be chauffeuring the kids or grandkids to their ballet classes, birthday parties, or soccer games. You might also be looking after an elderly parent. Perhaps you attempt to have date night once a week (okay, let's be real...make that once a month!) so you don't forget what your partner looks like. All this...*but for what?*

Purpose addresses the "for what?" question. It's what inspires you to jump out of bed every morning...what helps you stay sane and keep going when the road gets tough...what really engages you and fills you with excitement and enthusiasm.

Ian Percy, author of *The Profitable Power of Purpose* said, "Stop going to seminars on life balance. There is no such thing. The only way you're going to get balanced is if you are dead. What we all need to do is get clear about *life purpose*. Things that are balanced don't move and they're boring. Life is meant for teetering and tottering!"[1]

There's truth in that statement. Life balance is a great paradox.

In dance, "holding" a balance is just an illusion. It may seem like the dancer is poised perfectly still. But in fact, in order to achieve that illusion the dancer is in a constant state of movement, always adjusting this way or that. What stops her from falling flat on her face is how connected she is to her core. If she lets go of that, she will fall. And the riskier she "teeters and totters" the more connected she must be to her core. But that is where the excitement lies.

We'll talk more about this in Chapter 17. For now, realize that *your purpose is a key element of your CORE* and one of your most vital sources of enthusiasm. When you connect to your purpose you will be unstoppable.

What's Your Calling?

For me, dancing was a "calling" as much as a profession. In fact, I have often heard dancers say they never really felt they had a choice. There was a passion and purpose that burned in their soul and it *had* to express itself. Otherwise they may not have done what it takes to succeed. The lifestyle of a professional dancer is a very demanding and arduous one.

Perhaps that's why George Balanchine, the famous choreographer, said "I don't want dancers who want to dance. I want dancers who *have* to dance."

What are you called to do? What burns in your soul? What do you *have* to do?

One of my favorite dancers, Michael Flatley, who created Riverdance, said that he believes every person has one thing they just have to do, and for him it was dancing. He went on to say that it is in finding that one thing and in *engaging with it fully* that one becomes most dynamically alive.[2]

I agree completely, because your life purpose is your Soul's destiny. It's like a blueprint or plan for your life. That's why when we access it, it feels so *right*. And when we get off track, it feels like something is missing from our lives.

I meet with coaching clients, some of whom are working so hard to make their career or business a success. They may be doing very well financially. Perhaps they finally reached "the pinnacle" of their career and received the coveted position they always wanted with the corner office on the top floor. Or maybe the business they started has now been recognized by their industry and peers as being the "best of the best."

Yet instead of feeling engaged and excited about these accomplishments, they are miserable. They feel that they have lost themselves along the way. What started out as a passion has become their prison.

But how did they get so off track? How did they go from following their passion to feeling trapped by it? Often, they didn't take the time to figure out what they *truly* wanted, not only from their career or business, but also what they wanted from *their life*. No wonder their lights are on dim!

We all get so busy trying to balance work, family, and other commitments. In the process, it's important to step back from time to time and ask yourself if your life is taking you where *you* want to go…where *you feel called* to go. If not, what changes need to be made?

I'm certainly not saying this process is easy. It takes courage to admit, especially to ourselves, that we are not living in integrity with our deepest passions and joy. And it takes even more courage to do something about it. But it is only by taking these first steps that you can live a fulfilling and meaningful life…a life with Full Wattage.

So, why are you here on earth, at this time? What truly motivates you? What really makes you tick? What brings *you* energy, passion, and joy?

Still not sure? Don't worry. We'll continue to clarify this for you as we move on.

But before we delve deeper into your sense of purpose in life, I would like to dispel some myths and illuminate some truths about life purpose.

Myth #1 – Life purpose is a great mystery.

It's not! Life purpose isn't something you have to go "out there" to find. Clues to your life purpose are everywhere. They are in the things that capture your interest and attention, things that have an "energetic signature" for you, and certainly things that motivate and excite you. The qualities you admire in others can be indications of your own life purpose. You can even find life purpose clues in the things that frustrate, anger, or irritate you.

Myth #2 – Life purpose is a job description.

"If I could just find the *perfect* job, then I would be happy." Nope! Much as you might like to believe this is true, it's not. If your purpose in life is CORE to who you are, then it has to be much more than simply a job description. It must be an integral part of all that you do.

I have heard so many people complain bitterly about their job not being fulfilling. Meanwhile, opportunities to engage in activities that would be purposeful pass them by unnoticed. Then they leave one job for another, thinking they will be more fulfilled, only to recreate their dissatisfaction there. Nothing really changed. Yes, having a job or a business that aligns with who you are is important, but that is just one small step of the dance.

Myth #3 – Once I discover my life purpose everything will fall into place easily.

Getting clear about your life purpose is just the first step (though a *very* important step). Sometimes discovering your purpose becomes a catalyst for change, and change is not always easy. You often have to be willing to experience temporary discomfort as you build the life of your dreams.

So what *is* true about life purpose?

Truth #1 – Life purpose is much more of a journey than a destination.

It is more a state of being than a state of doing. It's about who you are and how you show up in the world. Your life purpose may be expressed in specific ways, including (hopefully) your career path. But essentially it is an ongoing journey.

Realize that the journey may not be a straight line from point A to point B. More often than not there are twists and detours along the path. And these unexpected "detours," although frustrating and discouraging at the time, can lead to the greatest insights about our purpose.

We often think that life purpose has to be this BIG thing. But again, to use the analogy of dance, what makes a good dancer might be their high kicks, super fast footwork, high leaps, or their ability to turn like a top. But what makes a good dancer great has less to do with the tricks and everything to do with how they fill the space between the movements.

Just like the quality of a dancer is determined by how he fills the space between the big movements, the quality of our life is determined by how we fill the space between the big moments of our journey. Remember, it's always about the journey.

When you think about the times in your life that you felt the greatest joy, it probably was not that once-in-a-lifetime vacation you took; most likely, it was found in a smile, a touch, a kind word...because you often find the most joy and meaning in the ordinary moments of life. The same is true of life purpose. How can you bring a greater sense of purpose to your ordinary moments? How do you fill out the "in between?" We will explore that shortly.

Truth #2 – Your life purpose is a driving force.

Have you ever made a New Year's resolution? Did you know that, on average, most folks have given up on their resolutions by Jan 7th? That's because often our goals are things we think we *should* be doing. We tell ourselves, "I should work out more." "I should eat better." "I should lose those 10 lbs." "I should watch less TV."

However, when your goals emerge from your sense of purpose in life, there's a much higher likelihood of you achieving them. And as a result, you will have much more satisfaction, enthusiasm, and well-being.

Truth #3 – Your life purpose is an organizing force.

Have you ever experienced the power of synchronicity? Most of us have at some point in our lives. When you are living in alignment with your life purpose you become more magnetic and attract all kinds of supportive people and resources to you in ways you could not have previously imagined.

Knowing your life purpose also helps you stay focused and make decisions that are in alignment with who you are and why you are here. It acts like a barometer for the spirit.

So, if life purpose is such a powerful force in your life, how can you lead a more engaged, more productive, and more *purposeful* life? It begins by clarifying what your sense of purpose is. And that's next.

CHAPTER 3

Discovering Your Life Dance

"Follow your dreams, because you wouldn't want it so bad if you couldn't have it. The universe gives you these dreams because you can have them. If you're willing to work for it, you can have anything you want."

MICHAEL FLATLEY, Dancer and Creator of RiverDance

S INCE KNOWING YOUR LIFE PURPOSE is foundational to living a life with Full Wattage, this chapter is devoted to helping you uncover yours. As such, it has a different format than the rest of the book. It is filled with provocative questions and a number of activities that will help you to hone in on what is truly meaningful to you. There are also some real-life stories to inspire you along the way.

So, are you ready to begin the process of clarifying your life purpose?

Great! Let's jump right in...

The Foundation of Your Success

The first step is to **define what success really means to you.** To get your creative juices flowing, here are some things past workshop participants have said about success:

- I know I'm being successful when I sleep soundly at night knowing I made a positive difference in someone's life that day.
- I know I'm being successful when I get paid well for doing what I love.
- I know I'm being successful when I feel at peace and happy.
- I know I'm being successful when I am being true to myself.
- I know I'm being successful when my home life and work life feel balanced.

So now it's your turn. How would you define a successful life? As you answer, think about success in *all* areas of your life, including career, relationship, family, fun, friendship, community, etc. (Don't forget that you can download the companion guide from the website at www.FullWattage.com/resources if you want more room to write.)

Think of at least five answers to the following:

I know I'm being successful when:

1. _____

2. _____

3. _____

4. _____

5. _____

Did you think of five answers? Good for you!

Earlier I mentioned that the clues to your life purpose can show up anywhere. Following are some questions and processes to help you go back and collect those clues. Later in the chapter we'll put all those clues together and draft a Life Purpose Proclamation. But for now, fill in the blanks as best as you can.

You will be able to answer some of the questions right away. Others may require some pondering. So make a start now and feel free to return to this chapter any time to add to what you have written.

Answering the following essential questions will help you uncover more about your purpose in life...

___What would you do with your time if you didn't have to work at all?

_____

_____

_____

_____

_____

_____

_____

_____

_____

__What would an ideal day in your life look like? In what ways would it be different from your life today?

_____

_____

_____

_____

_____

_____

_____

_____

_____

_____

__When you were a kid, what did you _really_ want to do or be when you grew up?

_____

_____

_____

_____

_____

_____

_____

_____

_____

_____

CASE STUDY

Mary's Story

When Mary was a child she wanted to be a dancer. But she wasn't interested in tap, or jazz, or modern; she specifically had her heart set on being a ballerina. Her mother enrolled her in classes when she was 7 and, at her insistence, bought Mary a little pink tutu that she practically slept in.

Mary loved to dance and would do so at any opportunity. Every time she heard music playing, she'd be shaking and moving, pliéing and pirouetting. And if there was no music, she didn't let that stop her.

But when Mary was 11, a terrible thing happened. She had a HUGE growth spurt and in one year went from being one of the smallest to the tallest girl in her class.

At first she thought it was fun that she was finally catching up in height with her friends, but she just kept growing. Soon she was a full head taller than even the tallest boy in her ballet class.

Mary vividly remembers the day her dance teacher took her aside and suggested that she take up tap dancing. The teacher said Mary was too tall and would never be a ballerina. Mary was devastated. Even though her mother encouraged her to keep dancing, Mary had already made her decision. If she couldn't be a ballerina, then she wasn't going to dance, period. And she didn't.

Fast forward to her early 40s, and Mary is working for a large law firm as a legal secretary and not loving life at all. She is now single (after a rocky divorce) and feeling very unattractive and unloved.

Some of the girls in the office went out every Tuesday night and they kept trying to get Mary to go with them, but she wasn't interested. She was not in the mood for having fun!

But they wouldn't let up, so Mary finally said yes. Julie (one of the receptionists who happened to live near Mary) picked her up and they drove downtown to a building Mary had never noticed before. It looked pretty drab from the outside, but when she walked inside she could hardly believe her eyes. There was a huge, beautiful wooden dance floor that took up most of the space, with just enough room for a row or two of tables around the outside, and a small bar. A few couples were already on the dance floor, clearly practicing their moves.

Then a woman who was obviously in charge walked to the center of the room. Mary could tell by the confident way she held herself and her graceful poise that she was a professional dancer. She instructed the women and men to form two lines facing each other. Mary's first dance class in over 30 years was about to begin.

At first she was nervous and awkward, and she felt totally clumsy. Before that night Mary had never even heard of a dance style called West Coast Swing. But after a couple of weeks of lessons she fell in love with it. Mary quickly remembered how much she had loved to dance as a child, and how, in some ways, it had seemed like something had been missing all these years. It was as if she was reclaiming a part of herself that she had left behind. She was coming alive again!

A year later Mary met her future husband, Jeff, at a dance and they've been dancing together ever since (in more ways than one). They are a perfect match for each other. Sometimes Mary can hardly believe how things have turned around. She still works at the law firm, but she is currently exploring other career options that align more fully with her sense of purpose. For Mary, life is good.

Reclaiming her childhood love of dance gave Mary a new lease on life. It filled her with joy and enthusiasm, and made her so magnetic that she attracted her ideal life partner. It also inspired her to come to me for coaching, to get support in making some other significant life changes. When we explored her life purpose, she found that expressing herself through movement and dance was core to who she was...and the key to her coming alive again.

Remember, your life purpose is a journey, not a destination. The clues to it are all around you. A big clue for Mary was in her childhood love of dance. What about you? Has Mary's story reminded you of something you loved to do as a child?

When I was a child I loved to:

_____

_____

_____

_____

_____

_____

_____

_____

_____

Now, here are a few more questions to get you thinking about *your* life purpose.

When have you felt most peaceful in your life?

_____

_____

_____

_____

_____

_____

_____

_____

_____

_____

_____

What are you most proud of having accomplished at this point in your life?

_____

_____

_____

_____

_____

_____

_____

_____

_____

What do you *really love* to do? What makes you feel most alive?

_____

_____

_____

_____

_____

_____

_____

_____

_____

_____

_____

__What specifically would you most like the people at your funeral to say about you?

_____

_____

_____

_____

_____

_____

_____

_____

_____

_____

Find Your Purpose with a Process

Now you've reflected on and answered several questions, here is the first of three processes to help you pick up additional clues to your specific purpose in life.

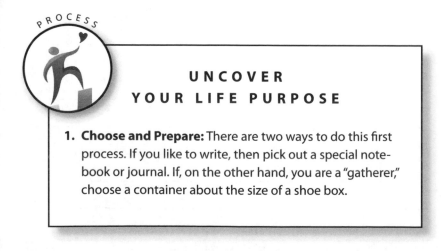

PROCESS

UNCOVER
YOUR LIFE PURPOSE

1. **Choose and Prepare:** There are two ways to do this first process. If you like to write, then pick out a special notebook or journal. If, on the other hand, you are a "gatherer," choose a container about the size of a shoe box.

2. **Collect and Capture:** Commit for the next thirty days to either write in your journal or collect in your box anything that grabs your attention and interest. Consider blog posts, websites, magazine or newspaper articles, comments you overhear people say in conversation, stories in the news, the titles of books you are attracted to, the names of songs or pieces of music you are drawn to, or names of people that intrigue you.

   Capture *anything* that gives you energy or that fascinates or piques your curiosity.

3. **Review and Summarize**: After thirty days, review your notes or your "collection" and see if there are any themes or common threads that emerge. Come back to this page and summarize your insights here.

   __Common threads that emerged are:

   _____

   _____

   _____

   _____

   _____

   _____

   _____

   _____

   _____

Diane's Story

Diane always loved music. However, as a music teacher and a musician, she often had to take assorted odd jobs to make ends meet. One of these jobs was a three-day temp position creating name badges for a magazine publisher's convention. She worked under the umbrella of the advertising department.

Diane did such a good job that the advertising department asked her to continue to work one day a week, on her day off from her teaching job. Diane agreed.

Then, at the beginning of the long summer holiday, Diane was offered, and accepted, a full-time summer position with the publisher.

And that's how Diane stepped into what ended up being a thirty-year career in advertising. It was never meant to be her "dream job," just something to tide her over while her music career took off.

Twenty years into her advertising career, Diane began to realize how disconnected she was feeling, but it would take her an additional ten years to finally be free.

The advertising industry is extremely high pressure and high stress, and the long hours were taking a toll on Diane's health. So she began to explore various avenues to health and healing, including shiatsu and massage. She even enrolled in a number of training programs to pursue *her developing interest in the healing arts, but the long hours that her work demanded meant that she never completed them.*

One day, her friend Francis said, "Diane I've found the perfect career for you." At first she didn't listen as she was tired of spending her money and vacation time taking classes she wasn't able to finish.

But her friend was insistent, so finally Diane signed up for a session of a healing modality called Guided Imagery and Music (GIM). GIM is a unique form of music therapy, and after one session, Diane was hooked and knew this is what she was meant to do. It was a perfect blend of music, which was her first passion, and her new found love of the healing arts.

However, for the next year, although Diane took regular GIM sessions, she resisted signing up for the first level of the training that would lead to her being a practitioner. She was concerned that work would consume her once again, and it would be yet another unfinished training she would begin.

So Diane was surprised one day when she received a notification from the training institute welcoming her to the program. She called them, excited yet confused. It turned out her brother, who had listened to her for a year saying that this is what she wanted to do, had registered her in the program and paid for her training. Diane cried...happy tears.

At first Diane managed, barely, to balance the require-ments of the training program with her demanding work schedule. But when it came to the third and final level of the GIM program, work once more took precedence, and Diane sadly watched as her classmates graduated without her.

Frustrated, tired, and deeply disappointed Diane hit her low point. She didn't see how she was ever going to free herself from a job that was eating away at her hap-piness. That was when she met with her counselor in the GIM program, who suggested to her, "Diane, have you thought of taking a sabbatical?" Immediately, Diane had a huge revelation. It felt as if the stars aligned, and in that instant, it was as good as done!

It took a little bit of planning, and it meant cutting back on some expenses for a while, but sooner than she ever thought possible Diane had a whole year to get her health back, complete her GIM training, and decide what was next.

And what was next? Well, Diane never did return to advertising. Instead, she finished her training and is now a Fellow of the Association for Music and Imagery. She currently has a thriving private practice that combines two of her greatest passions, music and healing, and is living with Full Wattage.

Diane's story of falling into a career by default and not by design is unfortunately not that unusual. It's one of the most common reasons people come to me for coaching. If you find yourself in a similar situation, *there are things you can do about it.*

Remember, living a purposeful life is about the journey, and there are many ways to get there. We just have to stay open to the possibilities. Sometimes amazing things can happen!

Let's move forward. Here are some additional questions to help you deepen your awareness of your purpose in life:

___What do you most love about your career or business?

_____

_____

_____

_____

___What changes would you most like to make regarding your career?

_____

_____

_____

___Who would you most love working with (an individual, group, or organization) and why?

_____

_____

_____

___ **Is there a particular business or volunteer project that you would be excited to work on or create?**

_____

_____

_____

_____

_____

You're doing great! Grab your notebook or journal. It's time for the second process that will help you get clarity about your life purpose. If you don't have time now, go and get your calendar and schedule it in.

PROCESS

20 MINUTES TO YOUR LIFE PURPOSE

1. **Solitude:** Find a quiet spot where you will be undisturbed for about twenty minutes.

2. **Center:** Take a couple of deep breaths to get centered and relaxed.

3. **Reflect:** Think about a specific time in your life when you felt deeply satisfied, fulfilled, engaged, alive, and happy. This can be from any period in your life, from your earliest memories all the way to the present.

4. **Capture:** Write down as many details about the experience as possible.

5. **Observe:** Take a minute or two to notice how you feel *now*. Often just thinking or writing about the times in your life that were purposeful can create feelings of calm excitement, enthusiasm, or peace. How about you?

6. **Repeat:** Repeat the whole process thinking about another experience and writing it down. Do this until your allocated time is up.

7. **Intention:** Repeat this process as often as you can for a period of thirty days. In fact, once you have set the intention to do this you might want to keep your notebook or journal handy. You never know when another memory will surface that you want to capture.

8. **Review:** Once again, review your notes at the end of the thirty day period and look for themes and patterns. Come back to this page and summarize your insights here.

__Common threads that emerged are:

_____

_____

_____

_____

_____

_____

Here are a few more questions for you to mull over...

___Who in history do you most admire and why?

_____

_____

_____

_____

_____

_____

___If you could wave a magic wand and solve a world problem, what would it be? And why is solving that problem important to you?

_____

_____

_____

_____

_____

___What was the most exciting thing that ever happened to you professionally or personally?

_____

_____

_____

_____

_____

PROCESS

TAP INTO
YOUR PURPOSE

This third process to tap into your life purpose will help you consciously access your intuition or your inner knowing. Remember, there is a plan or template for your life, and sometimes when we quiet our busy minds, that wiser aspect of ourselves can reveal that plan to us. It may come in whispers or it may come like a bolt of lightning. The important thing is to *listen* to that inner voice.

Allow yourself at least twenty minutes to do this process. Again, if now is not a good time, grab your calendar and block off the time to do it later.

Here is the process:

1. **Intention:** The first step is to turn off your phone if you are at home and let family members know not to disturb you. Realize that this may bring up issues about always being available every minute of the day. But it is important for your own wellbeing to occasionally "unplug" from all the demands around you. Trust that the world will manage without you for a short while.

2. **Inspire:** You may choose to play a piece of music that inspires you, or you may prefer silence. (If you would like silence, but your only option is a noisy environment, you can try a noise-canceling headset. They work quite well. I have also used a sound machine that created "white noise" and found it rather peaceful.) Or you may prefer to find a beautiful spot in nature, filled with natural sounds. Experiment to see what works best for you.

3. **Receive:** Sit comfortably, preferably with your back straight and supported so you can stay more alert.

4. **Rhythm**: Take a few deep breaths and relax. With each inhale, know you are feeding your brain with oxygen, which will enable clear and focused thinking. With each exhale, let go of any tension you are holding in your body.

5. **Invitation:** Consciously call in your own higher self, your inner guide, divine intelligence, pure inspiration, or whatever fits with your belief system. There is no right or wrong way to do this.

6. **Clarity:** Then, simply ask for clarity about your life purpose, your reason for being. Why are you here?

7. **Listen:** Be still and listen, listen, listen—not just with your ears, but also with your heart. Be open to what appears. If you find your mind wandering off track, know that is natural. Gently bring it back to focus on the questions: What is my purpose? What is my reason for being? Why am I here?

8. **Insight:** When you feel complete, write down any insights that occurred to you in your journal or notebook.

Repeat this process as often as you feel drawn to. Then, come back to this page and summarize your insights here.

__Insights that emerged are:

_____

_____

_____

_____

_____

Here are two final questions to help you clarify your sense of purpose:

___What aspects of your life do you feel are most on purpose for you? Think about what you are doing when you are happiest and most engaged in life.

_____

_____

_____

_____

___Why do you believe you are here on earth at this particular time?

_____

_____

_____

_____

Put It All Together

Now it's time to read through all of your answers to the questions in this chapter, as well as what you wrote in your journal or notebook. If you gathered materials, then review them again now. You are looking for any key themes that repeat or words or phrases that "jump out" at you.

The idea is to capture the essence of who you are and why you are here. With this awareness, you will then craft a working draft of your Life Purpose Proclamation.

To give you some ideas and inspiration, here are a few proclamation statements that clients and workshop participants have created:

- My purpose in life is to help others discover their purpose and manifest it in their lives.
- My purpose in life is to inspire joy and playfulness.
- My purpose in life is to be a catalyst for change and to support others on their healing journeys.
- My purpose in life is to nurture the animals.
- My purpose in life is to make people laugh.
- My purpose in life is to help youth manifest their potential, using the arts.
- My purpose in life is to bring people together in creative synergy.
- My purpose in life is to empower women entrepreneurs to create businesses that are sustainable for them and for the planet.
- My purpose in life is to spread happiness.

Now it's your turn to write your Life Purpose Proclamation. Don't worry about trying to "get it right" or about it being perfect. You can edit it at any time. As you go forward you may discover or remember more about yourself that you want to include in your Life Purpose Proclamation. So allow this to be a first draft that you can craft and refine.

Keep open to your possibilities. I've had clients who wrote their Life Purpose Proclamation very succinctly on the first try. Others found the need to write several drafts until it felt just right. Remember there is no right or wrong way to do this.

You can record your Life Purpose Proclamation on the following page.

___My purpose in life is to:

_____

_____

_____

_____

When you read your Life Purpose Proclamation and you experience a positive emotional response to it, you will know you are on the right track. For example, when you think about your Life Purpose Proclamation you may feel energized. It may evoke the feeling of being "at home." And if you find yourself saying, "Yes, this is me!" then you'll know you've got it right.

Once you have tapped into your sense of purpose, the next step is to weave your life purpose into all areas of your life, both at work and at home. That's the focus of the next chapter. Let's go...

CHAPTER 4

What's the Pointe?

"If you don't do your dance, who will?"

GABRIELLE ROTH, Movement Innovator

WITH YOUR WORKING DRAFT OF your Life Purpose Proclamation, you are now well on your way to living with Full Wattage! The next question to ponder is: "How can you integrate more of your sense of purpose into your daily living?"

The first step is to post your Life Purpose Proclamation somewhere you will see it often, such as on your bathroom mirror or next to your computer. Seeing the proclamation often and keeping it top of mind will help trigger ideas of how you can incorporate your purpose into your life, both at work and at home.

A fun (and often fulfilling) activity many of my clients and workshop participants have enjoyed is to create a unique, visual representation of their purpose, called a "vision board." You may also find this to be a great process to do with a number of your friends who are also exploring their purpose in life.

PROCESS

PICTURE
YOUR PURPOSE

1. **Picture This:** First, gather a number of magazines, preferably ones with lots of interesting images. I often find travel magazines are especially good for this. If you don't have many magazines, ask your local hairdresser or doctor's office. They are generally happy to pass some along. Local libraries often give away magazines they can no longer display or store.

2. **Gather Supplies:** You will need a poster board (one for each person if doing this with friends) and a glue stick, which can be purchased inexpensively from an office supply store. It's also good to have some colored markers handy in case you want to write on your vision board. And finally, get some scissors.

3. **Time for YOU:** Ideally, block off an hour or two when you will not be disturbed. If you don't have that much time, don't worry. You can do this in multiple smaller blocks of time if that is all you have. (You may be surprised by how quickly time passes when you are doing this.) Just make sure you have a shoe box, some large envelopes, or self-seal plastic bags handy to store your images in between sessions.

4. **Set the Stage:** You may enjoy having evocative music playing in the background, or you may prefer silence.

5. **Purposeful Inspiration**: Have your Life Purpose Proclamation handy so you can occasionally read it for inspiration.

6. **Open and Receive:** Set the intention to create a visual representation of your purpose, and then, let it go. In other words, let your intuition guide you as you go through the magazines and cut out any images you feel drawn to. Notice words that jump out at you and cut those out too.

   You may be attracted to some images that are literal representations of your purpose, and others where you don't see the connection at all. That's okay. Trust in the process and gather all the images that resonate with you.

7. **Coming Together:** The next step is to create a collage on the poster board with all of your images. You may choose to include words or not.

8. **Life as Art:** When you are done, be sure to hang your vision board someplace where you will see it often to remind you of your unique purpose.

You can see pictures of actual client vision boards at www.FullWattage.com/resources.

If you don't have space or privacy to display a full-sized poster board, you can use a scrapbook style method and create vision pages.

I had a client who created a journal-sized scrapbook that she carried with her to stay focused and motivated. It looked like a small business journal, but it was filled with photos and text that represented her life purpose, as well as her personal and professional visions and goals. She set up pages for each key area of her life. The journal could sit on her desk, and though she knew what it contained, others did not. This allowed her to maintain privacy in a shared space, yet stay in touch with what was most important to her.

Your Life as a Whole

Think about the different areas of your life. Consider:

- Career
- Friends
- Recreation
- Family
- Finances
- Community
- Relationship
- Spiritual
- Health
- Fun
- Contribution

To what extent are you already living your purpose in each of these areas? Following is a diagram you can fill in to give you a snapshot of how purposeful your life feels to you at present.

Dynamic Purpose Diagram

Look at the following image of a circle—what I call the Dynamic Purpose Diagram. If the center of the circle represents zero and the outer edge is a ten, on a zero to ten scale (with ten being the highest) fill in each wedge of the circle based on how purposeful that area of your life feels to you now.

You can also download this diagram in a larger format from www.fullwattage.com/resources.

Here is a completed example for you:

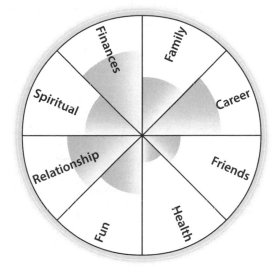

Now it's your turn. Here is a chart with the typical life areas identified. Mark your level of purposefulness in each area now.

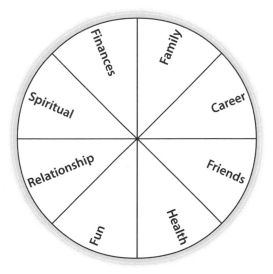

If you prefer, here is a blank Dynamic Purpose Diagram you can customize with the life areas that are important to you.

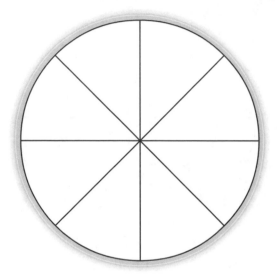

If you were completely living in alignment with your life purpose, how might these aspects of your life be different? What could you do to bring a greater sense of purpose into your day-to-day living?

Write down any initial insights you have here:

_____

_____

_____

To explore this further, let's take your career as an example, as your work is probably an important and necessary part of your life. It's also where you likely spend a significant percentage of your time. Do you see a relationship between your current career choice and your life purpose? In what ways, if any, does your career support your purpose?

__My career supports my life purpose by:

_____

_____

_____

_____

The connection between your career and your purpose may be obvious immediately, or it may not. If the latter is the case, don't worry. Perhaps with a little further observation you will see a connection. For example, you may be learning new skills in your current job that will be useful to you in your dream job. Or maybe your present position is helping you save enough money to go back to school and get the necessary qualifications you will need to pursue your life purpose.

CASE STUDY

Angie's Story

When Angie came to me for coaching, she disliked her job as a financial analyst for a large organization. She spent most of her day in a small office in front of a computer.

When we worked together to clarify her life purpose, what emerged was that Angie had a lifelong interest in the healing arts and had always felt that healing was her true purpose in life. However, as a single mom of two young children, she did not see how she could possibly manifest that in her current situation.

But when Angie did some research, she found that her local community college offered a massage therapy program. It had very flexible hours and would allow her to take classes around her children's schedule and her job. So she enrolled, and she absolutely loved every minute of it.

As she had limited time to attend classes, it took her twenty-four months to complete school and obtain her state massage license. But during that time she was happy because she was moving in the direction of her life purpose. Even her boss at work noticed her renewed energy, productivity, and enthusiasm. Living with clarity and focus energized her, even though she had a busy schedule. It all seemed to be "falling into place" for her.

Once she was licensed in massage, she approached her boss about reducing her schedule to four days a week, and on Fridays she did massage in a local day spa.

Now here is the interesting thing…Once she engaged her purpose, Angie began to enjoy her regular job more. Soon, people came to her for advice on natural healing. She even started regular brown bag lunch talks at work on health and wellness topics.

Angie now works three days a week at her financial job and is in private practice doing massage two days a week. Once her daughters are older she plans to go back to school to become a naturopathic doctor. Angie is definitely living with Full Wattage.

Here is what Angie's Dynamic Purpose Diagram looked like initially:

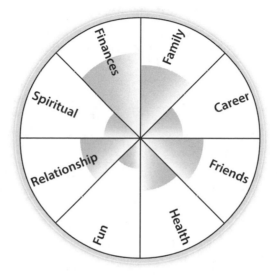

Here is what Angie's Dynamic Purpose Diagram looked like after she began living in alignment with her purpose.

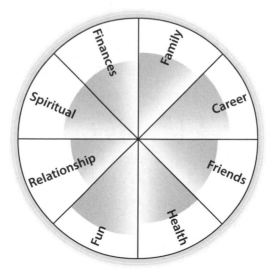

So, how about you? What are some steps you could take to incorporate more of your sense of purpose into your life? Take into account all the life areas that are important to you.

__To incorporate more of my purpose into my life I could:

1. _____

2. _____

3. _____

4. _____

5. _____

Quiet Contemplation

I'd like to suggest another important element to consider when you're trying to incorporate more of your sense of purpose into your daily living: Schedule time to quiet your mind for a few moments throughout your day. Then, set the intention to consciously connect to your CORE, and to your life purpose specifically.

When you quiet your mind, even briefly, you allow the flow of intuition to happen more readily. Therefore, disconnect from other distractions and allow the quiet to surround you. As you do, make sure you keep your notebook or journal handy for any insights you might get. Many of my clients are amazed at how powerful something as seemingly simple as this can be, and yet how hard it is to commit to. Like any new habit, it will take practice to develop, but I assure you, it is possible. I know you can do this!

As Alaina Love and Marc Cugnon wrote in *The Purpose Linked Organization*, "So many of us become immersed in the daily rigors of the work-day world, and we would say that there is little time for the luxury of Stillness and Contemplation. We think that we must be constantly available by phone or email or in person, and we fail to recognize the importance of scheduling a meeting with ourselves. We give most of our time to other things and other people in an effort to achieve."[3]

And yet these achievements often leave us empty. Remember, it's not just about the big moments, but about how we fill the "in-between."

CASE STUDY

Beth's Story

My client, Beth, would be the first to admit that she is often a little short on patience. Having said that, she generally arrives slightly late for her coaching sessions... and it's never her fault! However, she recently showed up on time (actually, even a tad early), and I could tell from the look on her face that she'd had a breakthrough.

Beth sat down and told me what happened. During her lunch break that day she decided to go to the post office, which was just across the street from where she worked. It was one of those sweltering hot and humid August days. Even though it was a short distance, by the time she got there she could feel rivulets of sweat running down the

*inside of her blouse. The post office did have air condi-
tioning, but it was not enough to cool her inner furnace.
And to make matters worse, there was only one counter
position open, resulting in a long line.*

*As Beth waited to mail her package she felt herself
getting more and more irritated. She thought about how
much time she was "wasting" and all the other things she
could be doing instead of just standing there. Then, just
when it was almost her turn, the gentleman in front of her
wanted to know exactly how a money order worked and
how it differed from Western Union. As the postal worker
patiently explained the difference (English was clearly not
the gentleman's first language), Beth found herself becoming more and more furious.*

*By the time it was her turn to be served she was ready
to explode. Unable to contain her anger, she vented all
her frustration at the poor guy behind the counter. She
demanded to know why they did not have more staff
working at lunchtime, as that was clearly one of the busi-
est times. She ranted on and on about how valuable her
time was, and that she had better things to do than to
stand around all day.*

*The postal worker listened until she was done. Then
he turned around and walked over to a little cloth cooler
sitting on a shelf. He unzipped it and lifted out what was
clearly a sandwich for his lunch. Then he pulled out a can
of soda. He walked over to Beth and handed the ice cold*

can to her saying, "You look like someone who could use a nice cold drink."

Beth was immediately disarmed by his gesture and accepted the drink gratefully. Then she looked into his eyes, really for the first time. What she saw was deep compassion. She thanked him, and in return he said, "My job is to spread kindness. Thank you for giving me an opportunity to do what I love."

Wow! As Beth described this to me, she had tears in her eyes. She was so impacted by one person's kindness that it transformed the rest of her day. She felt herself becoming kinder and gentler to her co-workers and employees as a result.

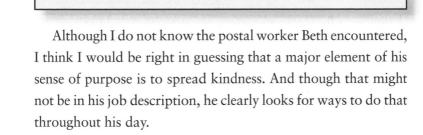

Although I do not know the postal worker Beth encountered, I think I would be right in guessing that a major element of his sense of purpose is to spread kindness. And though that might not be in his job description, he clearly looks for ways to do that throughout his day.

Again, it is not always the big things but the "in between" moments that often have the most profound impact, both for ourselves and others. So look for ways to fill your "in between" moments with purpose and your life will be richer and more deeply satisfying.

Your life purpose is your Soul's destiny—the blueprint for your life. When you engage with it your heart will be filled with joy, and you will experience courage, aliveness, and enthusiasm, despite the most challenging circumstances.

Finally, when you get off track (which happens to the best of us) you may feel like something is missing in your life. This is why taking quiet time to re-evaluate is so important. Determining your life purpose is not a process you do just once. It's something you want to take time to consider daily, weekly, monthly, or on special occasions—like your birthday or the New Year—to renew your commitment to living in alignment with your highest purpose.

You might decide to take a few minutes each evening before sleep to review your day and to ask yourself which parts of it felt most purposeful and why. If you find that the majority of your day did not feel purposeful, that might be an indication that something is off.

If you do find that you have wandered off track, don't worry. The important thing is to recognize that you need to make adjustments and then do whatever it takes to reconnect with your purpose, with your CORE.

Your CORE Brilliance

So let's review:

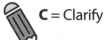 **C** = Clarify

__My Life Purpose is:

_____

_____

_____

_____

_____

_____

_____

O = Organize

___Three specific activities I commit to doing in the next thirty days to organize my life around my life purpose are:

1. _____

2. _____

3. _____

R = Release:

___Three things I am willing to let go of in order to live a more purposeful life are:

1. _____

2. _____

3. _____

E = Enthusiasm

When I do these things I know I will be more engaged with life and experience more energy, excitement, and enthusiasm. I will be on my way to living with Full Wattage!

Do What You Love
And Do Best!

Like a snowflake that falls from the skies, there is nobody else in this whole world exactly like you.

"There is a vitality, a life force,
a quickening that is
translated through you into action,
and because there is only
one of you in all time, this expression is unique.

And if you block it, it will never exist through
any other medium and be lost.
The world will not have it.

It is not your business to determine how good it is,
nor how valuable it is, nor how it compares
with other expressions.

It is your business to keep it yours
clearly and directly,
to keep the channel open.

You do not even have to
believe in yourself or your work.

You have to keep yourself open and aware
directly to the urges that motivate you.

Keep the channel open."

MARTHA GRAHAM[4], Dancer, Choreographer

CHAPTER 5

The Dance of Possibility...

"To dance is to be yourself. Larger, more beautiful, more powerful. This is power on earth and it is yours for the taking."

AGNES DEMILLE, Choreographer, Dancer

WHILE YOU MAY HAVE ASPECTS of your life or work that are quite purposeful, you may still find yourself involved in activities at work or at home that are simply draining and exhausting.

When you feel frustrated, depleted, overwhelmed, and stressed, it is often because you're spending too much time doing things outside of your natural strengths and preferences.

Throughout this chapter we will be talking about your natural strengths. Your preferences are related to your strengths, but they are slightly different.

When considering preferences, people often think of things like whether they prefer ranch dressing over blue cheese. However, in this case I am talking about something much deeper. Your preferences are connected to how you are "hard-wired" and dictate how you see and interact with the world around you.

For example…

- Are you a soloist, or do you function best as part of a team?
- Would you describe yourself as an "idea, big vision person," or do you have a tendency to focus on detail?
- Do you enjoy repetitive tasks, or do you find them boring?
- Do you have a knack for planning and strategy, or do you prefer spontaneity?
- Would you say that you are results and goal focused, or do you prefer a more "let's wait and see how things turn out" approach?
- Do you make decisions swiftly and decisively, or do you prefer to "mull things over"?

There are no right or wrong answers to these questions. Your answers are simply indications of your natural preferences and are precursors to your strengths.

It might surprise you to know that your natural preferences (often referred to as your "style") don't change much through-out your life. That's why it's important to get as much clarity about them as possible. (I'll share with you a resource that will help you do that later in this chapter.)

When you find yourself spending a great amount of time doing things *outside* of your preferences and strengths you will often feel tired and irritated, because you are engaging in activi-ties that weaken you versus strengthen you.

On the other hand, focusing on activities that utilize your natural preferences and strengths will energize you and keep your enthusiasm levels high. Remember, your strengths are another key element of your CORE.

Now that we have talked briefly about preferences (you can learn more about them at www.fullwattage.com/resources), it's time to define a strength.

According to Donald Clifton and Marcus Buckingham, authors of *Now Discover Your Strengths*, a strength is something you do with "consistent, near-perfect performance."[5] But there is a lot more to the story than that. They also said a strength is something that you enjoy, that feels easy for you, and that makes you feel good. You might even lose track of time when you do it since you are doing something that is in alignment with your natural preferences.

On the other hand, a weakness is not just something you're not good at; *it actually robs you of energy.* For instance, I decided that in order to save money I would do my own bookkeeping. So I purchased an accounting program and hired someone to customize it for my business. They also taught me bookkeeping basics.

As it turned out I was very accurate when it came to balancing the books. There was just one problem: I really disliked doing it. I found bookkeeping boring and tedious. After half a day of inputting information from receipts and balancing the accounts, I felt exhausted. It totally zapped my energy. As a result, I kept putting off doing it, and the piles of paperwork mounted up around me.

Eventually the mountains of paperwork created so much stress that I decided to hire a bookkeeper. The first time she showed up in my office I could hardly believe how fast she was. My new bookkeeper easily accomplished in a couple of hours what it would have taken me days to do. And she seemed to *love* doing it! It actually *gave* her energy.

In fact, numerous studies show that when people focus on their strengths, not only are they happier, but they actually perform *much* better too. Gallup, an organization that has studied and researched human behavior for over seventy-five years stated that when people operate from their strengths, not only are they more effective in the workplace, but they are also six times more likely to be engaged in their work. In addition, these same people are three times as likely to report having an excellent quality of life.[6] Now that sounds like the kind of workday I want to have. How about you?

See the Good Through the Bad

Recently, someone asked me, "If something starts off challenging but you work at it and it gets easier, is that really a strength?" The answer is…it depends. Clifton and Buckingham went on to explain that there are three aspects to a strength:

- First there is the innate talent you are born with (which is connected to your natural preferences).
- Then there are specific skills (which are like the steps of a process).
- And third, there is knowledge. [7]

In other words, I could teach you the skill, or the steps involved, in doing a pirouette. You could gain the knowledge of good body mechanics and the proper time to turn your head.

But the innate talent to spin like a top...well, you either have it or you don't.

Choreographer George Balanchine said:

"One is born to be a dancer. No teacher can work miracles, nor will years of training make a good dancer of an untalented pupil. One may be able to acquire a certain technical facility, but no one can ever acquire an exceptional talent. I have never prided myself on having an unusually gifted pupil. A Pavlova is no one's pupil but God's."

Well said!

Think about some of your innate talents. Not sure what yours are? Just like with your life purpose, look for clues. Your natural talents often show up at a young age and can even be things you were criticized for.

As a child, whenever I wanted to do something and was told it couldn't be done, I would generally have many suggestions for alternate ways it *could* be done. I drove my mother and teachers crazy with my ideas. Consequently, one of the things I heard most often was "Elizabeth, you are always so full of good ideas." It was said with a good dose of British sarcasm and was *not* meant as a compliment.

But guess what? It's true! I am always full of good ideas. I love to brainstorm with people and help them find unique solutions to problems they are having. This has turned out to be a huge asset in my career as a coach, facilitator, and professional speaker.

How about you? What were you most criticized for as a child?

___As a child I was most criticized for:

1. _____

2. _____

3. _____

Our natural talents are also hidden in the things we criticize ourselves for. Think back to childhood. As kids, when we have a unique ability or stand out in some way, we often criticize ourselves because we want to be normal and fit in. We criticize ourselves and others for being different. But our strange idiosyncrasies are often clues to our strengths.

For example, think about the kid in school who always asked tons of questions and seemed to bug everyone with an unquenchable curiosity. Would it surprise you to learn that this child grew up to become a sought-after forensic specialist? Likewise, the child who was highly competitive and argumentative might now be using those skills in the courtroom as a prosecuting attorney. Of course, these scenarios may never happen if children get hung up on criticizing themselves.

The pressure to conform or simply "get along" makes it difficult to hang on to the very aspects of our lives that make us unique. Yet these qualities may be the keys to your innate strengths. So what did you most criticize yourself for as a child?

___As a child I most criticized myself for:

1. _____

2. _____

3. _____

Consider the possibility that all the things you ever thought wrong with you actually hold the keys to your greatest gifts and strengths.

For example, have you ever known you could do something quite well but, despite that, you still had a nagging feeling that you're just *not good enough*...so you held back?

But what if you took that thought and flipped it around 180° so you could see what is right about you? For instance, people who suffer from "I'm not good enough" actually have the innate ability to see something at its *highest possibility*, including traits about themselves. The twist is they think they should be that way *now*. And by comparison, they tell themselves that they are not good enough.

But their strength is that they will constantly strive to be better. They are never complacent. People who struggle with not feeling good enough are never satisfied with mediocrity. That's what is *right* about them. All they have to do is trust that they will get there and know that where they are is perfect *in this moment*.

So the next time *you* tell yourself that you're not good enough, stop and reframe it. Remind yourself that in this moment where you are is perfect. Then look at where you are (your current reality) as well as where you want to be (your ideal vision), and know that you are on a journey toward reaching that goal. Many of the tools and processes I have already shared with you will help you close that gap. I'll be sharing plenty more in upcoming chapters.

With that said, look at the things you wrote down that you were criticized for, or that you criticized yourself for, and see them from another perspective. What might your hidden gifts and talents be?

My hidden gifts and talents are:

1. _____

2. _____

3. _____

Speaking of gifts and talents, I was recently watching a TV show called *Live to Dance*. It was a contest to find the best dance act in America. There was a troupe of young male dancers who made it to the finals and they were amazing.

During an interview, one of the dancers (who had a lot of gymnastics training but not a formal dance background) said that if he had focused on how little dance training he had he would not have made it so far. Instead, he focused on the things he could do that were unique to him—his strengths as a gymnast.

As part of their training, dancers learn to play to their strengths. Some dancers may get amazing height in their jumps and appear to just hang in the air. Others have the ability to master complex and precise footwork, while some have wonderful flexibility or great musicality. A good choreographer knows how to work with the dancers' natural strengths to bring out the best in them and in the troupe.

In fact, the success of that dance troupe on *Live to Dance* was in large part due to the choreographer's ability to watch each dancer and see what they were *really* good at, and then to maximize that.

A great dance company does not get to be great because all the dancers are well-rounded individuals. That would be so boring. A great dance company is one in which the varied styles and strengths of the dancers are enhanced. They come together in a choreographed, cohesive whole.

What Are Your Natural Strengths?

You may not have the luxury of a choreographer watching over you and pointing out your strengths, so here is an exercise that has helped many of my clients. It might help you, too.

PROCESS

HAPPY JAR, GRUMPY JAR

1. **Create:** Begin by taking two jars or small baskets (or some type of container). Tape a smiley face on one and a grumpy face on the other.

2. **Prepare:** Put the containers on your desk or someplace easy to access, along with a pile of small pieces of paper or a pad of sticky notes.

3. **Record:** For a period of five days, every time you engage in an activity or task that excites, inspires, or energizes you, or where you lose track of time, briefly write what you were doing on a piece of paper and put it in the happy jar.

   Conversely, every time you do something that makes you feel tired, bored, angry, irritable, or frustrated, write the activity down and put it in the grumpy jar.

4. **List:** After five days take the pieces of paper out of each jar. Create two lists, one with everything you wrote on the papers in the grumpy jar (your grumpy list), and the other with everything you put in the happy jar (your happy list). If you wrote an activity down more than once and put it in a jar, make a note on your list of how many times the activity showed up.

5. **Review:** Take a look at your lists. The activities on your happy list are BIG clues to your natural strengths. And those on your grumpy list are clear indications of your weaknesses. Pay particular attention if an activity showed up more than once.

___ **Now it's time to toot your own horn. Go on, don't be shy. My greatest strengths, both personally and professionally, are:**

1. _____

2. _____

3. _____

What are the areas you have a hard time with? What activities drain you? Remember, a weakness is not just something you aren't good at, but something that robs you of your energy too. It weakens you, *even if it is something you do well!*

___**The activities and tasks that zap my energy are:**

1. _____

2. _____

3. _____

If you would like help in this area I highly recommend an online assessment that will help you identify your natural preferences and tendencies, your motivators and preferred work environments, as well as your typical reactions to stress and pressure. I use this assessment with almost all of my clients and have found it to be amazingly accurate.

In fact, it's not unusual for clients to tell me they are both surprised and relieved by what this tool reveals. They often say, "No wonder I've felt like I've been struggling and out of sync. Now it all makes sense!"

You can learn more about this assessment, as well as online and live workshops I offer utilizing this and other tools, to help you gain deeper insights into your strengths and preferences at: www.fullwattage.com/resources.

Now, is it realistic to expect that 100% of your day can be spent doing the things you love and are naturally good at? Probably not. But what if you took steps in that direction?

___What are five things you could do to incorporate more of your strengths into your day?

1. _____

2. _____

3. _____

4. _____

5. _____

Organizing your life around your strengths and natural talents may not happen all at once. But you can incrementally move toward doing more activities that play to your strengths each week.

Fill a Need and Feel Fulfilled

Remember, you have unique strengths, talents, and abilities that nobody else has. Consider the possibility that somewhere on this planet there are people with needs that *exactly* match your talents. They can not have their needs met by anyone else as well as you.

For every talent there is a need in the world. When you find a need that matches your talent and fill it, not only does that expand your heart, but it also releases tremendous enthusiasm.

Wouldn't you agree that it feels good when you have the opportunity to express your gifts and talents in a way that serves others? And when you don't express them you often feel out of balance, irritated, and restless. I often relate it to a pressure cooker with the release value closed. When the steam is not allowed to be released, the whole thing explodes.

Perhaps you have a job that is not fulfilling and that may even be zapping your energy. If so, you are not alone. Out of the more than ten million workers Gallup has surveyed over the past decade, only one-third of them believe that they have the opportunity to do what they do best every day at work.[8]

One of the best ways to turn that around and increase your sense of meaning and contribution at work is to look for a need that engages one or more of your natural strengths or talents, and just do it! Do it simply because it is your gift to give, without being attached to the results.

Besides, you don't always know how your actions might influence someone's life for the better. Many people can recall a teacher, friend, mentor, or even a total stranger who reached out and shared their gifts at a key moment. Often, they never knew the impact that their actions had on the other person.

Here's an example: my first year living in America was both exciting and challenging. I had moved to New York City with very little money, and when Christmas rolled around I didn't have the resources to fly back to Scotland. I missed my family terribly.

I was in a rocky relationship at the time, and my dance career was not taking off as quickly as I'd hoped. All in all, I was very down emotionally.

One morning while taking my regular modern dance class with the wonderful teacher and choreographer, May O'Donnell, another dancer whom I hardly knew approached me. She said that in addition to dancing (she danced in May's company) she was also a massage therapist. She noticed I looked a bit down and wanted to gift me a massage. I was so taken aback by her kindness.

I graciously accepted her gift. A few days later I took the subway to the end of the line, to her massage studio, and I received one of the most loving and nurturing massages I've ever had in my life (and since then I've had quite a few). I had been stuffing my feelings so as not to feel the pain of loneliness, and as a result I was feeling disconnected (from others and from myself). She helped me to open my heart again.

As I was leaving she handed me a bag of oranges and wished me a Merry Christmas. I thanked her very much for the massage (and the oranges).

Soon after the holidays her dance company went on tour. Then she moved on to dance with another company so I no longer saw her in class. Unfortunately, I never had the chance to tell her the impact her kindness had on me. To this day I vividly remember the kindness of someone I hardly knew—someone who reached out to me at a very difficult time in my life and made things a whole lot better.

I now look for ways to "pass it on," and when I do, it fills *me* with joy.

So no matter how mundane your life may seem at times, never underestimate the power of sharing your unique gifts with others.

By finding as many ways as possible to express your strengths, gifts, and talents in your day-to-day life, not only will you perform at your best, but you will also experience a new depth of satisfaction and joy. And you'll have more energy, excitement, drive, and enthusiasm. You will be living with Full Wattage! I don't know about you, but I am all for that.

Reclaim Your Strength!

Don't end up like the coaching clients who have come to me over the years because they felt burned out, in the wrong business or the wrong jobs, and were ready to make drastic changes. Often, it was not that they were in the wrong job at all; it was that they were doing the *wrong tasks and activities*. They were not engaging their strengths and doing the things they did best and loved to do.

Fear and pride can keep us from stepping out and fully expressing our innate gifts and talents. This occurs when we have been ignoring our talents for so long that we actually begin to feel awkward about claiming them.

Instead we continue working on tasks that deplete and weaken us versus strengthen us. However, if you don't get to the CORE of the issue and build your life around your gifts, you will most likely end up recreating the same burnout in your next position.

Living in suppression and resistance can be *very* fatiguing, as it takes lots of energy to keep something repressed.

So remember, never let the demands of your job or of other people pull you away from focusing on the things you enjoy and are naturally good at. If you do, you may find yourself feeling tired and turning to artificial sources of energy, like excess coffee, sugar, or energy drinks. You might even turn into an adrenaline junkie. We'll talk about that in more depth later.

Since you'll always be living and working with others, you'll always be dealing with their perspectives, assumptions, and even their schedules. It's up to you to determine how much power their opinions and perspectives will have in your life and in the choices you make.

If other people *are* making unreasonable demands on you, then it might be time to fire the judges in your life! That's sometimes the only way to reclaim your innate strengths so you can live *your* life with greater purpose and meaning.

CHAPTER 6

Fire the Judges!

"The seed of doubt is poison."

BRUNO TONIOLI, Choreographer, Judge on Dancing With The Stars

Now THAT YOU HAVE CLARIFIED your sense of purpose in life, as well as your natural strengths and talents, you will be unstoppable, right? Maybe, but not so fast...

When I was dancing on the SS Uganda, trying (not very successfully) to keep my balance, at first all I could think about were the two talent scouts sitting in the middle of the second row. I felt them judging every move I made, and that made it impossible for me to be fully present—to be my enthusiastic and authentic self.

It took the wise voice of Rick, the program director, to break the fearful hold of doubt. He firmly reminded me to connect to my CORE. In this case it related not only to the physical core of my body, but also to the deeper core of my purpose and passion as a dancer, to my natural talent, and to my value of giving 100% of myself to my audience no matter what else might be going on (rocking boat and all!). In that moment I realized that I did not have to be at the mercy of what anybody else thought. So I fired the judges, and I just *danced*.

A few years later, when I was about to graduate from a prestigious dance academy in London, I encountered another clash with self doubt. I was in the office of one of my dance teachers for a career counseling session. As I sat on the other side of her very large and imposing oak desk, I felt so nervous that my palms were sweating. As we neared the end of our time together I finally got up the courage to ask her my most important question: "Do you think I've got what it takes to make it as a professional dancer?"

She looked me up and down, saying nothing. Then after a long silence she replied, "It depends."

"On what?" I asked.

"On whether *you think* you've got what it takes to make it as a professional dancer."

Once again I was reminded of how easy it is to give away our power to someone else. I was inviting her to be another judge and tell me whether I was going to be successful. Thank goodness she didn't accept that role!

I find it interesting how often we manipulate ourselves to try to win the approval of others, whether it is our parents, our boss, our peers, or someone else, even as adults.

Who are the judges in your life? Who do you give your power away to? Are you waiting for someone to tell you that you are good enough? That you are worthy enough? That you are deserving?

__The biggest judges in my life are:

1. _____

2. _____

3. _____

Fire the INNER Judge

Interestingly, the most critical judge I had to fire on the SS Uganda wasn't either of the two sitting in the audience. It was the one inside of *me!* Often, our greatest challenge in awakening to our brilliance is to move beyond our own self-doubt and judgment.

As Marianne Williamson wrote in her wonderful book, *A Return To Love: Reflections on the Principles of A Course in Miracles*:

> *"Our deepest fear is not that we are inadequate.*
> *Our deepest fear is that we are powerful beyond measure.*
> *It is our light, not our darkness that most frightens us.*
> *We ask ourselves, Who am I to be brilliant, gorgeous,*
> *talented, fabulous?*
> *Actually, who are you not to be?*
> *You are a child of God.*
> *Your playing small does not serve the world.*
> *There is nothing enlightened about shrinking so that other*
> *people won't feel insecure around you.*
> *We are all meant to shine, as children do.*

We were born to make manifest the glory of God that is within us.
It's not just in some of us; it's in everyone.
And as we let our own light shine, we unconsciously give other people permission to do the same.
As we are liberated from our own fear, our presence automatically liberates others."[9]

So why do we listen to our inner judge—that critical voice that chips away at our self-confidence? Why *don't* we let ourselves shine? Why *don't* we base more of our lives on our strengths and natural abilities and confidently pursue our dreams?

I think it's because most of us have been taught to focus on our weaknesses, not our strengths. Think about it...when you were in school, what was given the most attention—the subjects you naturally did well in, or the one thing you got the D minus for?

Instead of focusing on our strengths we are taught to develop our weaknesses so we will be well-rounded individuals. No wonder we become our own worst critic! And so begins the vicious cycle of self doubt, which perpetuates the notion of not being good enough.

The "not enough" syndrome stifles people every day. In fact, it can hold people back for years when not dealt with head on. I work on this issue with clients frequently and am always glad to see when our work can help them break free of the cycle. Not that I am immune to it myself...as they say, "You teach what you need to learn."

As a child, I spent years trapped in the "not enough" syndrome due to my weight. You see, I have always been thin, but when I was a kid I was downright skinny. I couldn't put weight on no matter how much I tried. At one point the doctor told my mom to give me Guinness. But then again, he was the same doctor who told her to give me warm milk with honey and whisky at the first sign of a cold. Hey, it worked!

At school during recess, the boys would come limping over to me shouting, "I'm a pirate and I'm searching for your sunken chest!" Yep, you couldn't make something like that up.

But the worst part of all was my skinny legs. The teasing was bad enough in primary school when I could at least wear thick socks practically up to my knees. But when I moved to high school, the uniform rules dictated that young ladies had to wear fine nylon stockings. I was mortified. I felt so exposed. I would actually wear three or four pairs of stockings at a time, but it didn't make any difference.

I got so tired of walking down the hallway and hearing, "Liz, Liz stop! You've got a couple of threads hanging from your skirt...Oh sorry, that's your legs."

But as much as I felt judged by others, I was my own worst enemy, and I grew to be extremely self conscious of my skinny legs.

What's your story? What happened to YOU? What incidents helped form your image of yourself? What did you hear from others? And what did you tell yourself as a result?

___The three key incidents that influenced my image of myself were:

1. _____

2. _____

3. _____

____**What I made up and told myself as a result was:**

1. _____

2. _____

3. _____

Visualize Your Ideal Story

Each of us has an image of who we are, and that image will be the greatest determining factor in our success or failure in *every* area of our lives.

Unfortunately, that image is primarily built by our failures, weaknesses, and disappointments. Why? Because your brain actually gives *higher priority* to negative experiences over positive ones. Yes, that humiliating experience you had when you were thirteen is stored in a part of the brain that is easier to access, and therefore easier to remember, than all the good things that happened to you. (I'll explain more about the latest research on the brain in Chapter 10.) As long as a negative self-image controls your mind, you will never be truly successful.

Fortunately, I had a vision. Despite my skinny legs I dreamed of being a dancer on the stage. But I didn't want to dance on just any stage. I had a specific stage in mind: Carnegie Hall, New York City.

As young as I can remember I would climb up on the kitchen table with my little tap shoes on and announce to anyone who happened to be around, "It's Liz Fletcher!" Then I would tap dance my little heart out on the table. In no time at all the kitchen would disappear, and I was on stage at Carnegie Hall. I'd feel the heat of the lights, see the smiling faces in the first few rows, and hear the people clapping and cheering. But it wasn't just a silly daydream—it was a scene I truly believed.

Visualization is a powerful tool because the mind can't tell the difference between what is real and what is imagined. In fact, if you ever find yourself stuck, it's possible that an old self-image has surfaced and your mind thinks it is real. So what do you do to get rid of it? I'd like to share with you a process I use with my clients. Though simple, it has proven to be very effective. Use this process whenever you find yourself in a rut or in an unresourceful place.

PROCESS

SWITCH

1. **Breathe:** Begin by taking a couple of deep, full breaths. I know it can be hard to motivate yourself to do this when you are really stuck, especially when your body feels lethargic. But give it a try. You might be surprised by how a few simple breaths can shift your energy.

2. **Assess:** Take a moment to assess the reality in which you currently find yourself. What are the circumstances? What are you telling yourself? How do you feel?

3. **Opposites:** Now imagine the polar opposite of the situation you are in. What might that look like, sound like, feel like?

4. **Switch:** Visualize yourself in that new situation. See yourself exactly the way you would like to be. Put yourself in that new reality in your mind's eye. The more vividly you

can imagine it, the more powerful it will be. Take as much time as you need with this.

Some of my clients have even found it useful to say the word "switch" to themselves when they step into the new reality in their mind's eye. It helps to reinforce the new and let go of the old.

You can repeat this process any time you feel the old images returning. With enough practice, you'll soon replace those images of failure with images of success. By doing this visualization exercise regularly you will destroy the thoughts that hold you back. That's powerful!

Additionally, as you change the image you have of yourself into a more successful one, you will become energized and more magnetic. Yes, you will actually attract all kinds of people and situations into your life to help you in unexpected ways. Here's what happened to me...

When I was in my early twenties I was living in New York City, studying with some of the greatest modern dancers of all time. One day a photographer friend called and asked if I was interested in doing a photo shoot for one of his clients. The project was a book cover for a novel about a ballerina, and they needed a picture of a pair of dancer's legs. So I agreed.

The next thing I knew I was paying my New York City rent and expenses on income I was making *as a leg model*. In fact, as irony would have it, one of my clients was a large hosiery company and my legs adorned the packages *of thousands of pairs of ladies stockings.* I often wondered if any of those packages ever made it to my hometown in Scotland. What would those kids think now if they knew my skinny legs had become such an asset?

And in case you're wondering, yes, my greatest visualization from childhood did eventually manifest, and I made it to Carnegie Hall. As I stood on that famous stage on the opening night of my dance performance I wondered if, perhaps, I was standing in the very same spot that Tchaikovsky had stood, or Judy Garland, or even the Beatles! And as I soaked in the applause, I remembered all those times as a child when I had fiercely visualized that *exact moment.* Imagine how different my life could have been if I had let self doubt stop me from living my dreams.

What about you? Do you have any dreams that you are holding back?

Three dreams I have that have not manifested *yet* are:

1. _____

2. _____

3. _____

Remember, our biggest challenge in awakening to our brilliance is to move beyond our own self-doubt and judgment. What's true about you is that *you are magnificent beyond compare.*

So don't worry about how many times you have failed or what you have done in the past. Your past does not have to determine your future.

The movie *Billy Elliott* makes this point beautifully. In the movie, Billy is the young son of an English coal miner who has fallen on hard times. His dad encourages Billy to take up boxing, but Billy's unexpected love of dance leads him to ditch his boxing gloves and trade them for ballet slippers. Even though he knows his family and friends will judge him harshly if they found out about his dancing, Billy doesn't let that stop him.

There is a great scene in the movie where Billy breaks loose in the street and dances his heart out. His enthusiasm and love of dance are contagious. By the end of the movie his family recognizes his talent and supports his dream of being a dancer. Ultimately, Billy goes on to become a leading dancer in the West End of London.

The message is clear: Don't get hung up on what people think about you, because in reality you cannot control that. What they think about you is *their* business. Don't spend your life dancing for the judges. Show up on the stage of your own life totally present and alive with Full Wattage!

Are you ready to *fire the judges in your life*...especially if the biggest one is YOU?

It's time to get bigger about who you are! The next chapter will show you how.

CHAPTER 7

Step it Up! Get Bigger About Who You Are!

"I'm always telling dancers that you're not defined by the end of your fingertips, or the top of your head, or the bottom of your feet. You are the expanse. You are the infinity."

JUDITH JAMESON, Artistic Director Emerita, Alvin Ailey American Dance Theatre

W HEN WE ARE FEELING STRESSED and overwhelmed in life, it's easy to see ourselves as that struggling, small self. We can get stuck in this limiting view.

But who you are and what you are capable of achieving is so much more than that. And it's the challenges and struggles in life that help us evolve into all we are capable of becoming. That is how we manifest the beauty and power within us.

Just look at the life of any "Great One" and you will quickly realize this is true. Very few (if indeed any) achieved greatness without facing trials and challenges.

Often they had to stare their failures in the face and not let their lack of visible success stop them.

They prove this simple secret to success: Do not identify with the part of you that is small and struggling. Step outside of the limited view of who you are. Remember that you are magnificent beyond compare. That is the truth about who you are.

It doesn't matter if you don't believe that truth *yet*. Over time, it's possible to build a successful, joy-filled, expansive, abundant, happy, enthusiastic self-image. As you do, you will notice profound changes in your life, because how you view yourself greatly impacts *every* area of your life.

Here's a wonderful example of the power of holding a bigger vision of who you are.

CASE STUDY

Brendon's Story

Brendon Burchard is the founder of Experts Academy, and is both a New York Times and USA Today best-selling author. He teaches people how they can make a difference and make money sharing their message and their expertise.

However, when he was just getting started in his business he lived in a tiny apartment in San Francisco, living on cheap burritos. He used a three-legged table that was a cast-off from his mother's sewing room as his desk.

Brendon was totally broke, yet he was writing about success. He had a powerful message to share, and he knew it would make a difference in many people's lives. But every so often he would find himself doubting that anyone would care what he had to say about success.

At those moments he would tell himself, "Brendon, yes, you are starting out small, kid; everyone has to... You are going to help millions of people some day. Today is the day; you just keep working at it. You are bigger than this stupid apartment because your dreams have no boundaries."[10]

Brendon understood the importance of getting bigger about who you are. He later said, "You need to have a grander vision of yourself...despite your present circumstances, which will propel you into action and achievement."[11]

Brendon now earns millions of dollars helping others make a difference and make a living by sharing their knowledge and advice.

So take a lesson from Brendon: Any time you find your mind dwelling on an image of yourself that is too small, keep bringing your attention back to your unlimited, expansive self.

Claim Your Victories

Banishing self-doubt and focusing on your potential can be challenging, especially when you're in the thick of obstacles. Following are some practical things you can do to help with that. Adding some (or all) of these activities to your life will support you in overcoming your self-doubt, increasing your confidence, and rebuilding your self-image into one of success.

It's time to step it up, get bigger about who you are, and live with Full Wattage!

From Visualization to Actualization

In the last chapter I mentioned visualization and shared a process called Switch, which is one of the most powerful ways to change your self-image and replace negative thought forms with positive ones. So remember to take time each day to visualize how you would like to be. Here are a few questions to help you focus:

- How would you like to be physically, emotionally, mentally, spiritually?
- What is your ideal body image?
- Are there any emotional qualities you would like to develop?
- What about mental or spiritual attributes?

(I have a short audio recording of a visualization process you can listen to or download from www.fullwattage.com/resources.)

The more you visualize your ideal self image, the more you will actualize it in your life. This doesn't happen as a result of wishful thinking; it happens because you are activating and releasing the inner potential that is currently dormant within you. You are waking up your CORE. You are creating yourself anew from the inside out!

Another powerful activity is to start a "Victory Journal." Here's how:

VICTORY JOURNAL

1. **Beauty:** Begin by choosing a notebook or journal *just for this purpose*. Pick something that uplifts and inspires you. You can even start with a regular, inexpensive notebook and glue a beautiful photograph or a picture from a magazine on the cover.

2. **Rhythm:** Set aside a few minutes each day for the process—five to ten minutes is plenty. The end of the day is an especially good time to do this, but the best time for you will be a time that you can commit to regularly.

3. **Victory:** During the time you've set aside, write in your journal all of the victories and successes you had that day. Whether the victory is big or small, include it.

   Maybe you got up twenty minutes earlier to exercise. Or perhaps you took care of that difficult phone call you have been putting off. Maybe you said "no" to that big slice of chocolate cake. Your victories will be unique to you and your current situation.

   As you do this, you might also recall past successes you have had. Write those down, too.

4. Celebrate: Now take a minute or two to absorb what you have written, and allow your successes to really soak in. Congratulate yourself for your victories!

5. Review: Every so often, particularly when you are having a hard day, go back through your journal and read about the successes and victories you have accomplished. This is a sure way to increase your confidence, boost your self-esteem, and get bigger about who you are.

C A S E   S T U D Y

Josie's Story

My client Josie had a very negative self-image. The fact that she was overweight and unhealthy greatly contributed to her mindset. I suggested that she take a few moments each day to think about and write down all the times in her life when she felt energized, healthy, vitally alive, and really good about herself—even going back to when she was very young.

It was remarkable what a boost this gave to Josie's image of herself. As a result, she started walking to work instead of driving, she stopped eating refined sugars and replaced them with fresh fruit, and she joined a local gym and began swimming three times a week. After three months she had dropped twenty pounds and looked great! Just doing this simple Victory Journal process helped her take the necessary actions to create a healthier lifestyle.

But Josie isn't the only one who had success with this process. Perhaps the story of my client Emilie will resonate more with you.

CASE STUDY

Emilie's Story

Emilie had the very common habit of procrastinating. She was deeply frustrated with the disappointing cycle of committing to something and then putting it off. It was also hurting her graphic design business, as she wasn't completing tasks in a timely manner. She began coaching with me in order to break that cycle.

Emilie, like most people, would think of all the things she should have been doing but wasn't, and then would mentally "beat herself up" over it. So instead of engaging in that negative mindset and consequently poor self-image of herself, I asked Emilie to think back to all the times in her life when she took positive action on something. She then wrote about them in detail in her journal.

It was amazing the difference this made! Emilie began by setting more realistic goals for herself that she could actually follow through on. She finally gave her own website a makeover (something she wanted to do for two years), and she filed away the piles of papers that were gathering on her desk. Emilie then hired a student to input the information from all those business cards she had gathered at networking events into a database, and she began to follow up with the potential clients.

Emilie found it much easier to tackle those tasks she had been putting off when she had a more favorable image of herself.

This Victory Journal process works because reflecting on past successes encourages us and gives us hope. It raises our energy, which enables us to take positive action. This can help us break free of those self-defeating patterns, like procrastination.

What about you? What are some of your past victories and successes? Start recording them in your journal and review your notes on a regular basis.

To get you started, what are three victories or successes you have had so far today?

Three victories or successes I've had so far today are:

1. _____

2. _____

3. _____

Remember, by bringing your focus to your successes you are helping to build a new and more positive self-image. At the same time you are destroying the underlying image that may be holding you back. And that's powerful!

Have the Courage to Let Go

In order to build your confidence and get bigger about who you are, you sometimes need to let go of all the relationships that are undermining you.

Poet and corporate consultant David Whyte said, "Anything or anyone that does not bring you alive is too small for you."[12] Well said!

But letting go of a relationship can be hard. You may have loyalty to someone who was there for you in the past but is now bringing you down.

Or perhaps a cherished family member, your esteemed boss at work, or even a close "friend" is undermining you the most. In those situations, you might have to start by taking small steps to distance yourself.

CASE STUDY

Maria's Story

Maria and Judith had been best friends since elementary school. During their senior year of high school, Judith said she'd like to become a dental assistant, and Maria decided that was the career path for her too. So they researched colleges together and picked a program they both liked.

After graduation, Maria and Judith both found jobs in their hometown and continued to spend a lot of time together. After a few years Maria decided she wanted to go back to school and become a dentist. She shared this news with Judith, along with her dream to someday have her own pediatric dental practice.

Much to her surprise, Judith was the first person to try to talk her out of it. She told Maria that she didn't think she had what it took to run her own practice. Judith also said she was doubtful about Maria's ability to complete the rigorous training to become a dentist.

Maria was shocked by Judith's reply but she took steps toward her dream anyway. As she did, she noticed that Judith became more and more undermining. Eventually Maria began to doubt herself. After all, Judith knew her so well. Maybe she was right!

Maria's confusion led her to seek out coaching, and we began working together. It became clear early on that Maria was passionate about having her own practice, and she felt that working with children was her "true calling." She also met the qualifications needed to apply for dental school.

I explained to her that sometimes when people take big steps toward their dreams, others in their lives often get scared that they will be left behind. I thought this might be happening with Judith, and as a result she was undermining Maria's choices.

Maria decided to talk to Judith to reassure her that their friendship was important to her, and that her going to dental school would not change that. But despite her best efforts, Judith continued to criticize and undermine Maria every chance she got. Finally, even though it was difficult to do, Maria started spending less and less time with Judith. When it came time to choose a dental school, Maria opted for her first choice, which was in a different state.

Maria is still sad that things turned out the way they did with Judith, and she keeps hoping that someday Judith will come around. However, she confided in me that she would be even more devastated if she had given up on her dream in order to maintain her friendship. Today, Maria is doing very well in dental school and already has a business plan in place for when she graduates.

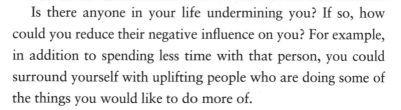

Is there anyone in your life undermining you? If so, how could you reduce their negative influence on you? For example, in addition to spending less time with that person, you could surround yourself with uplifting people who are doing some of the things you would like to do more of.

Let's say you wanted to start a home-based business, but like Maria, you had a naysayer in your life. In this example, you might consider finding a group of entrepreneurs who you could have regular communications with. Most towns and cities have networking groups for business owners, and some are even specific for women business owners, African American business owners, Latino business owners, etc.

It's also helpful to release any attachment you have to convincing the naysayer you are right, and to let go of the need for their approval. These last two points may take some practice.

What if the person is someone you have to interact with regularly, like a family member or co-worker? Then, be prepared! Plan in advance how you can change the subject if it turns pessimistic. Practice switching the conversation to a neutral topic or to something they are interested in. Whatever you do, avoid getting pulled into their web of negativity. In other words, be clear about your expectations around this person, and don't allow yourself to be seduced into conversations you know will lead down an undermining path.

And watch out for *The Hopeful Stupid Pattern*. This pattern occurs when we allow ourselves to be drawn into a situation (again!) because we are hopeful it will be different this time. However, we are stupid to think this, as there is absolutely no evidence to back that up. The Hopeful Stupid Pattern is responsible for more disappointment than any other. So be discerning and have boundaries in place. Know when to say "no."

When you absolutely have to interact with someone who is a naysayer, plan an activity to do immediately after the interaction that is uplifting, like calling a good friend. You don't need to talk about what just happened; simply have a conversation that will help shift the energy. We'll talk more about this in Chapter 15.

If you have to interact with someone who tends to undermine you, think about some of the actions you can take to negate their influence.

__Three steps I can take to reduce the undermining influence of _____ (fill in their name, or a nickname that only you will know) **in my life are:**

1. _____

2. _____

3. _____

Forgive Yourself

In forging a more positive self-image it's also important to forgive yourself for failures and past mistakes you've made, and move on.

This step is crucial, because we often do to others what we do to ourselves. In other words, when we have not fully forgiven ourselves for something, we often judge others *for that very same thing.*

Allow me to illustrate: I used to be an extreme perfectionist. If I got 99 out of 100 in an exam, I'd be mad at myself for getting an answer wrong. I was hard on myself and equally as hard on others who didn't do something the way I thought it should be done.

Focusing so much on mistakes (mine and others) was a blueprint for a negative self-image. I had to learn (and am still working on it!) how to forgive myself for my "imperfections" and see the beauty of being a "work in progress." Once I started this practice, I noticed that I was much less judgmental, not just of myself, but of others, too.

___ What past mistakes or failures do you most need to forgive yourself for?

_____

_____

_____

_____

___ What do you most judge others for?

_____

_____

_____

_____

Get Inspired

One great way to improve your self-image is by watching, reading about, or listening to uplifting and inspiring true stories of other people's successes, especially of how they overcame difficulties. In fact, begin a list of inspirational materials you can turn to when you need a boost. Why not start that now!

___ My favorite inspirational books, movies, and materials are:

_____

_____

_____

_____

(Go to www.fullwattage.com/resources for more ideas of inspirational books, movies, and other materials you might enjoy.)

Reward Yourself

Reward and celebrate your successes no matter how small they may seem.

Each time I finish writing a chapter of this book, I have a cup of my favorite tea that I savor for special occasions. It's not so much the tea itself; it's *the intention, the anticipation,* and *the enjoyment* of the ritual that's special.

What would you like to celebrate? Maybe it's getting a new client, making a sale, getting a raise, waking up early to exercise, landing that ideal job, or simply doing a task you have been putting off.

How would you like to celebrate? To give you some ideas, here are some things my clients and workshop participants do to celebrate:

- Go for a walk in a beautiful place.
- Have a latte.
- Call a friend and share the success.
- Enjoy a special glass of wine they may not normally buy.
- Block off time to do absolutely anything they want.
- Have a nice meal out.
- Purchase a book from their wish list, or order it from the library.
- Have a bubble bath.

How about you? What will you celebrate and how will you celebrate? Remember, it's about the intention, the anticipation, and the enjoyment. Have fun!

What I Will Celebrate: **How I Will Celebrate:**

_____   _____

_____   _____

_____   _____

PROCESS

REWIND
THAT MOVIE

Here is a powerful process you can do at the end of each day to help transform your self-image.

1. **Prepare:** Each evening, just before you settle down for sleep, sit with your back tall and straight. You can lean against a wall or sit on a chair if you need support. It's recommended that you don't do this lying down—you don't want to fall asleep.

2. **Breathe:** Take a couple of full, deep breaths to calm your mind. Focus your attention on the inhale and exhale as much as possible.

3. **Review:** Review your entire day. Was it all perfect, or was there something you did that, in retrospect, you wished you had done differently? If everything you did through-out your entire day was perfect, congratulate yourself and enjoy a great night's sleep. Otherwise, continue.

4. **Observe:** If there was something you wished you had done differently, see the incident or the activity in your mind's eye. Maybe you said something you later regret-ted, or you reacted to something without thinking of the consequences. If there was more than one incident, pick

one to start with. You can always come back to another one later.

Observe that moment with as much detail as possible. What is it about the activity or the incident that you wish you had done differently? (Note: Only focus on things you did, said, or felt that *you have control over.* You can't control or change something that someone else did!)

As you observe, stay as detached as possible. I know this is not easy, but imagine you are watching a movie. In this movie you are just an actor saying your lines and going through the motions.

5. **Rewind:** In your mind, rewind the movie and play it again, but with a new ending. See yourself being the way you would have liked to be. How would you have liked to react? What do you wish you had said? (Remember, this is about replacing negative thought forms with positive ones. This is not the time to practice all the things you'd love to say to your boss or that client from hell. That's a different exercise.) See the new ending in as much detail as possible.

6. **Repeat:** You may want to replay this new movie more than once. So, when you get to the end of the new movie, imagine hitting the rewind button and play it again. Do this as often as you need to until the new ending over-shadows the old one in your mind.

7. **Relax:** When you are done, take a few more deep, focused breaths and relax. If you want to transform another incident, go back to step three and repeat the process from there. When you are done, have a wonderful sleep.

This process seems simple but is amazingly effective at changing your self-image into a more positive one. Realize

that it takes practice to hold the new image of your preferred response in your mind without it wandering. Stay
with it and you will be rewarded with greater confidence
and well-being.

Of course, you are still accountable for what you did or
said. But this is a powerful step to change your self-image
and to support you in making more positive choices next
time.

Help Others to Help Yourself

Without a doubt, one of the greatest ways to improve your
self-image is to help other people improve theirs. A kind word
can go a long way in someone's life. In fact, Mark Twain said he
could live for two months on one good compliment! So let your
family, friends, and co-workers know how much you appreciate
them.

Studies show that appreciation is more important to people
than money and promotions.[13] Mary Kay Ash, business woman
and founder of Mary Kay Cosmetics, said, "There are two
things people want more than sex and money—recognition
and praise."

Therefore, find ways to appreciate others and watch your
own self-image blossom.

To start, pick three people in your life who you think could
use a little appreciation.

__Three people I want to show my appreciation to are:

1. _____

2. _____

3. _____

You can do many things to show your appreciation, and most don't cost much, if anything. You could mail a hand-written card, make a phone call, send an email to the person's boss stating what a great job he or she is doing and copy that person on it, send a gift card with a note, give a flower, or leave an appreciative voice message when you know there's no one there to answer. You will be amazed at the difference such a simple act can make for the recipient...and for you.

Make the Commitment

You now have a number of techniques at your disposal that will help you boost your confidence and improve your self-image. The most important thing is to pick a few and just start! Of all the things I've mentioned, which activities do you commit to focusing on now to improve your self-image?

__I commit to:

1. _____

2. _____

3. _____

Congratulations on making that big step toward improving your self-image. Keep taking action and you'll soon notice your confidence increasing as you get bigger about who you are. Now it's time to return to your CORE.

Your CORE Brilliance

We began this section discussing your strengths. Let's review and summarize.

C = Clarify

___ **My greatest strengths are:** (Remember, get bigger about who you are.)

1. _____

2. _____

3. _____

O = Organize

___ **Three specific activities I commit to doing in the next thirty days to organize my life around my strengths are:**

1. _____

2. _____

3. _____

R = Release:

___ **Three things I am willing to let go of in order to focus on my strengths and gifts are:**

1. _____

2. _____

3. _____

E = Enthusiasm

When I do these things I know I will experience more energy, excitement, and enthusiasm in my life. I will be well on my way to living with Full Wattage!

What Matters Most...

Your values dictate your entire
attitude toward life.
Do you know what your
core values are?

CHAPTER 8

Dancing From the Inside Out

*"Some (wo)men have thousands of reasons why they cannot
do what they want to, when all they need is
one reason why they can."*

MARTHA GRAHAM, Dance Innovator, Choreographer

YOUR VALUES ARE AN INTEGRAL part of who you are. If you didn't have the values that you have, your entire attitude toward life would be different.

However, your most important values, your top two or three, should be absolutely non-negotiable. I call these your *core values*. At all times, but especially when the floor is rocking in your life, your core values will be your anchor in the storm.

Do you know what your core values are?

When you are crystal clear on what your core values are, you have a concrete and tangible way to make decisions.

Have you ever known someone who was indecisive, seemed confused, kept changing her mind, or continually made decisions that did not support her? That happens when we are not clear on what our values actually are.

Here is an exercise to help you get crystal clear about your core values.[14]

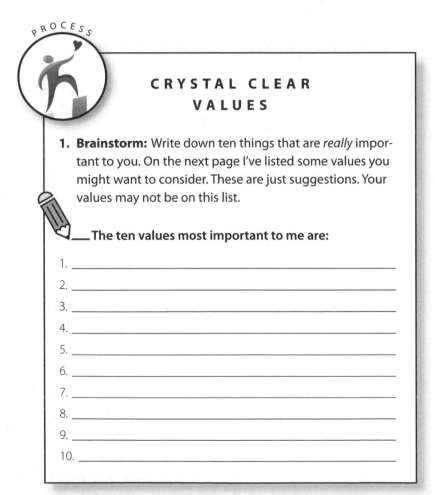

CRYSTAL CLEAR VALUES

1. **Brainstorm:** Write down ten things that are *really* important to you. On the next page I've listed some values you might want to consider. These are just suggestions. Your values may not be on this list.

___The ten values most important to me are:

1. _____
2. _____
3. _____
4. _____
5. _____
6. _____
7. _____
8. _____
9. _____
10. _____

Accomplishment	Honesty	Play
Advancement	Independence	Pleasure
Adventure	Innovation	Power
Affection	Integrity	Pride
Altruism	Intelligence	Privacy
Appearance	Joy	Purposefulness
Balance	Leadership	Recognition
Beauty	Learning	Risk
Challenge	Love	Security
Clarity	Loyalty	Self-Respect
Community	Mastery	Service
Cooperation	Order	Spirituality
Creativity	Ownership	Stability
Family	Passion	Variety
Freedom	Peace	Vitality
Friendship	Personal	Wealth
Health	Development	Wisdom

2. **Eliminate:** Next, put a line through the five values on your list of ten that are the *least* important. When you have finished this step you should be left with your top five values, not in any particular order.

3. **Write:** Get five small pieces of paper. On each piece write one of your top five values. You should end up with five pieces of paper, with one of your top five values written on each.

4. **Arrange:** Take the pieces of paper and lay them in front of you. Rank them in order of importance. Then number

them from one to five, with number one being the *most* important value and number five being the least.

5. **Decide:** Take value number five (least important) and value number four and put them side by side. Ask yourself, "If I had to give up value number five for value number four permanently, would I do it?" You have to answer "yes" or "no" — "maybe" is not an option!

6. **Illuminate:** If the answer is "yes," move up and ask the same question in regard to value number four and value number three. Again, you have to answer "yes" or "no."

If the answer is "no," put down value number four, and ask yourself, "If I had to give up value number five for value number three, would I do it?"

Continue this process, each time putting down the value you would give up and holding onto the one you would not give up. You will eventually end up with the one value that truly is the most important to you.

7. **Clarify:** Once you have completed step six, re-number the values in order of their true importance to you.

___ **My top five values (in order of importance to me) are:**

1. _____

2. _____

3. _____

4. _____

5. _____

Did the order of your values change from step four to step seven? For most people, the answer is "yes." Many times we think something is important to us, but when forced to make a choice between one value and another our true values emerge.

Was it hard for you to choose between some of your values? Maybe you struggled giving one or more of them up? Here is a little secret: When you get the order right, you will find that your number one value *includes all your other values;* therefore, you don't feel you are giving anything up. Your number one value is all inclusive.

The Crystal Clear Values process is a great exercise to do with a partner. Having someone else ask you to choose between your values can be very revealing. Your partner is a witness to your process, and that is powerful. Just having them present will change the dynamics. Try it!

It's also more difficult to cheat when you have a partner. Sometimes, when we don't want to give a value up, we try to find a creative way to keep them both. I've had clients who did this process on their own make up new words that combined two or more values because they couldn't decide between them! Having a partner remind you that you have to choose *one* value each time can help you be more decisive. Your partner can also encourage you when you get stuck. That's why I highly recommend you have a friend or a coach do this process with you.

Of all the processes I do with clients and workshop participants, the Crystal Clear Values process is one of the most profound. Why? Because clarifying your values and taking a stand for them in your life is essential for maintaining personal integrity. And it's only when we live in alignment with our deepest values that we experience high levels of energy and enthusiasm. People who feel exhausted and burnt out are often out of sync with their own values.

If you would like further support in clarifying your values, I have an excellent tool on my website. You can find it at www. fullwattage.com/resources.

Get Organized

Clarifying your core values is the first step. (Remember the "C" in CORE.) The second step is to *organize* your personal and professional life around these values so you give them the time and energy they deserve.

We often think that to feel balanced, fulfilled, and enthusiastic we have to give equal time to each area of life. But that is simply not true. A balanced life is one in which the areas that are most important to YOU are given priority.

When you look at how you spend your time, or where you focus your energy, is it a true expression of your most cherished core values?

For example, you might say that your spouse or your kids are the most important thing in your life. But you continually take on projects at work that keep you away from them. Or, maybe variety is important to you, but you're stuck in an all-too-familiar routine. Or you might really value friendship, yet when you review your calendar you have no space for social activities. If you don't prioritize your values in your life, then it's impossible to experience joy and enthusiasm on a regular basis, because something deeply important to you is not getting attention.

So what happens when you say something is important to you but your actions do not support that? Take Fiona...

CASE STUDY

Fiona's Story

Fiona came to me for coaching because she needed help making some lifestyle changes, especially when it came to her health. Fiona said that health was her number one value. Both her parents had health challenges that prevented them from doing many of the activities they had hoped to enjoy when they retired. Fiona did not want that to happen to her. However, she consistently worked long hours at a job she loved, didn't take time to exercise, and her diet was horrible. No matter what goals she set for herself to support a healthy lifestyle, she sabotaged them by her daily choices.

Together we did the Crystal Clear Values process...and her results surprised us both. The value that ended up in the number one spot was not health, but vocation. And number two was contribution to society (which she saw as interrelated with her work). This was a huge "ah ha" moment for Fiona. And it felt so right.

Then we discussed the various ways she could nurture her top two values. One of the first things Fiona realized was that she would not be able to continue to do the work she loved if she did not take better care of herself. That inspired her to start going to the gym regularly, to improve her diet, and to make sure she got sufficient rest and relaxation.

> *Before, Fiona had been sabotaging her efforts to stay healthy because she was motivated by fear (of becoming unhealthy like her parents). But once she got in touch with what she really valued, she had all the drive she needed to follow through with her health and fitness goals. And she was able to sustain that enthusiasm for the long term. Now she had clarity and was able to go forward utilizing Full Wattage.*

As Fiona shows, when you really connect to something you value, you need very little outside motivation to stay focused. However, when you don't see or feel the value of something, doing it will seem difficult no matter how much you try to motivate yourself to take action. The same is true if you are operating from fear.

If you are having a hard time following through with the things you say are important to you, *stop*! Take a really good look and see if the things you say are your top values really are in the right order. I am continually surprised by how many people have a "feeling sense" regarding their core values, but they are not able to clearly articulate the specifics. Second guessing can lead to subordinating your core values, and that will lead you down a stressful path.

Or maybe, like Fiona, it's a matter of shifting your perspective about something so it does fulfill one of your top values. Doing that can make a task or activity you currently find tedious more enjoyable and effortless.

Additionally, knowing your values can help you during those tough decision making times—those times when you can't determine which of two options would be the smarter move. Consider what happened with my client Gail...

CASE STUDY

Gail's Story

Gail wanted to change her career and was very unhappy at her current job. The big question was, "Should she quit without having another job lined up, or should she stay (even though she was miserable) until she had another plan mapped out?"

While Gail had enough financial reserves to quit her job and take time to explore her options, the values of "spontaneity," "risk," or "adventure" were nowhere close to her top five. In fact, her top value was "security." If she had left her job without having her next step lined up, she would have experienced a lot of stress. She eventually did make the move, but she did it gradually and in a way that honored her value of security.

Both Fiona and Gail are perfect examples of why you need to get clarity about your values and then organize your life around them. Doing so will *absolutely* lead to a more meaningful, focused, and goal-fitting life filled with joy and enthusiasm. That's another secret to living with Full Wattage!

Go back now to page 134 and review *your* top five values. Are any of them not currently getting the attention they deserve in your life?

___ **The following values of mine need more attention:**

1. _____

2. _____

3. _____

___ **Activities I could incorporate into my life, or changes I could make to honor my top values, are:**

1. _____

2. _____

3. _____

So far we have explored what your top values might be, as well as how to organize your life around them. But you're not done. It's also important to re-assess your values from time to time to make sure you haven't fallen out of sync. Continue on and let's explore this idea next.

CHAPTER 9

Getting Back in Sync

"Learning to walk sets you free. Learning to dance gives you the greatest freedom of all: to express with your whole self the person you are."

MELISSA HAYDEN, Prima Ballerina, NYC Ballet

IN ORDER TO LIVE AN enthusiastic and joy-filled life you have to first *clarify* your values. The second step is to *organize* your personal and professional life around them to give them the time and energy they deserve.

Unfortunately, we often find ourselves in situations where we have drifted away from what's important to us. At those times we need to step back and re-evaluate our values and priorities.

The warning signs that you're not living in sync with your values are usually clear...if you listen. You may dislike your job or feel irritable and unhappy. Perhaps you have a hard time sleeping, or you want to sleep all the time. Maybe you feel dis-satisfied, disengaged...and you're just not having fun.

That's when you know it is time to revisit your CORE. Otherwise you might get an unwanted visit from the Meter Man...

When I was nine years old, my parents separated and we left our lovely big house on a hill. My mom, my siblings, and I moved into a sixth-floor walk-up attic apartment. It was *not* in the best part of town.

We were totally broke. Even so, when my mom's friend John told her he knew of a way to fiddle the electric meter so we would get free electricity, my mom was horrified and refused to do it. And while some of the apartments had both gas and elec-tric, ours was all electric, which was very expensive. At times there just was not enough money to go around.

The financial strain got the best of my mom and she finally gave in to John's idea. He came over the next day to show her how to rig the meter. He warned her only to do it at night because the meter men came around to read the meters in the daytime and early evening. If she got caught *she would go to jail.*

At first she did it reluctantly, and very sparingly, always late at night. But soon winter came, and with it, shorter days. As the temperatures dropped and the kids got colder, mom got bolder and started tweaking the meter earlier and earlier.

One evening we were eating dinner when suddenly my mom's face went white. She jumped up and shouted, "Liz, turn out the lights and come quickly. Everyone else....BE QUIET!"

I followed her into the bathroom (which was really just a tiny closet with a toilet), and then I heard it too....the thump,

thump, thump of heavy boots on the stairs. Then I heard a deep, booming voice shout, "Meter!!!" The meter man was in the building. It would not take him long to get to us.

The electric meter was above the toilet, which you had to stand on to reach the meter. However, there was a window high up on the bathroom wall that looked out onto the landing. It put you in full view of anyone coming up the stairs, *if you happened to be standing on the toilet with the light on.*

It was dark. Mom got up on the toilet seat, and I stepped up beside her. She handed me a small flashlight, which I held, while she took the cover off the meter and tried to "un-rig" it.

Thump, thump, thump! The Meter Man was making his way up the stairs. He was getting closer and closer. Just one more floor and we would be in full view.

Meanwhile, I had visions of my mom being taken away to jail and all of us kids being sent to an orphanage. I had been reading *way* too many novels.

Right then my youngest sister started to wale. I hissed at her, "BE QUIET." Mom, getting more nervous by the minute, dropped the screwdriver. I gave her the flashlight and scrambled down to get the screwdriver when I heard his big, heavy boots coming up the final stairs.

I gave mom the screwdriver. She closed the cover, turned the final screw, and snapped off the flashlight. We quickly huddled down below the window. The only sound was that of my heart pounding.

Then I heard thump, thump, thump as he came up the last steps...and went right past our door to the neighbor's flat. He banged on her door and yelled, "Meter...Gas!"

GAS!?!

I thought my mom would have been relieved that it was the gas meter man and not the electric meter man. I thought she'd be smiling at the relief that she was not going to jail. But when I looked over at her, she looked sad and exhausted. At the time I didn't know why. All I knew is that from that day on, my mom never touched the meter again.

It wasn't until years later that I understood. It wasn't the fear of getting caught that troubled her the most. It was that my mom's core values are integrity, responsibility, and honesty. Every time she turned that meter off, it went against *everything* she valued, which slowly eroded her self-worth and her joy. She knew she wasn't being true to herself and that someday it would catch up with her. The meter man coming was simply a self-fulfilling prophesy.

Stay True to You

What does the "Meter Man" represent in your life? Are there any areas where you are giving away your power because you are not being true to yourself? Be honest.

__Areas I know I'm not being true to myself are:

1. _____

2. _____

3. _____

In *every moment of every day* we are constantly prioritizing one value over another. What we say is important to us is not always reflected in the choices we make. But it is impossible to be balanced, fulfilled, and live with enthusiasm when one or more of our core values are being compromised.

Once you compromise one of your values, you often find yourself on a slippery slope. Therefore, no matter how much the floor is rocking in your life, don't sacrifice your values. If you do, you will discover that living out of sync with your values has cost you your energy and your joy.

Your CORE Brilliance

Let's review:

C = Clarify

__ **My top values are:**

1. _____

2. _____

3. _____

O = Organize

__ **Three specific activities I commit to doing in the next thirty days to organize my life around my top values are:**

1. _____

2. _____

3. _____

R = Release:

___Three things I am willing to let go of in order to live in alignment with what matters most to me are:

1. _____

2. _____

3. _____

E = Enthusiasm

When I do these things I know I will experience more energy, excitement, and enthusiasm in my life. I will be well on my way to living with Full Wattage.

Living With Full Wattage!

*Why settle for anything less than
being fully, dynamically,
enthusiastically alive?*

CHAPTER 10

Attitude!

"You have to leave all excuses on the side of the stage."

NIGEL LYTHGOE, Producer (So You Think You Can Dance),
Choreographer, Dancer

W E HAVE EXPLORED THE THREE key aspects of your CORE, and now I have a question for you. If living a purposeful, strengths-based, values-driven life is such a great thing, what's stopping you from doing it? What stops you from fully experiencing enthusiasm, joy, and significance in your daily life? What stops you from living with Full Wattage?

After years of working with many clients and workshop participants, I have found the three biggest saboteurs that keep people from living with Full Wattage. I'll share them with you now.

Saboteur #1 – Your own beliefs.

We already discussed how your beliefs affect you when it comes to your own self-image. But what about other areas of your life?

Think about your beliefs regarding work. We often view our work as a necessary evil. Our goal simply becomes to get through the day or through the week. We hear common sayings like, "Thank God it's Friday!" and "Living for the weekend." Many people can't wait for retirement.

A recent survey showed that only 45% of Americans are satisfied with their jobs…and that figure is on the decline.[15] But is it right to spend such a great portion of our lives doing something unfulfilling at best? I don't think so.

So what are your beliefs about work?

__My beliefs about work that may be undermining my joy and enthusiasm are:

1. _____

2. _____

3. _____

Where did these beliefs come from? Often, they came from the things we heard as kids. What are some of the things you heard or observed growing up regarding work?

__Three things I overheard, was told, or observed about work were:

1. _____

2. _____

3. _____

Did your list include any of the following:

- "You have to work hard to make a living." Just like Donna Summer sang, "She works hard for the money. So hard for the money..."[16]
- I was lucky that my family supported my choice to become a dancer, but many of my friends were told, "Get a real job." Ouch!
- "It is selfish to have work you love."
- "Someone has to take out the garbage." The underlying belief here is that if everyone only did what they loved, nothing would get done!

Maybe it's time to call some of those limiting beliefs into question. More on how to do that in Chapter 12.

Saboteur #2 – Thinking that you must have complete clarity before you act.

I have often heard clients say, "Once I know for sure what my life purpose is, then I will start looking for a new job." They feel they have to know *exactly* what their purpose is before making any changes. But by waiting for that light bulb moment, they often end up stuck exactly where they are without moving forward.

When you are not sure, take steps in the direction you feel most drawn to and *clarity will come*, one way or the other. Even negative feedback helps you make different decisions and moves you forward.

Sometimes we become attached to focusing on confusion as an excuse not to take that next step. Or we spend so much time "preparing to prepare" and "fixing to get ready" that we never get out of the gate. Don't let that happen to you!

Saboteur #3 – Focusing on the negative.

It's amazing how much time we spend worrying about things that have not happened yet, and that probably won't *ever* happen.

You might find your self-talk confirming that you are always going to be stuck or that you cannot afford to make changes. Maybe you think if you try something new and fail, you will have ruined your future chances.

When you get caught up in negative self-talk you are simply awfulizing. (aw·ful·ize • v. [tr.] to imagine (something) to be as bad as it can possibly be.)[17]

More about that in a minute, but first...

What would you say are the three biggest saboteurs (be specific) that are getting in the way of *your* life feeling more purposeful and aligned with your strengths and values?

__My three biggest saboteurs are:

1. _____

2. _____

3. _____

Remember, no matter what the situation, you have a lot more control than you think. When I was on the SS Uganda, struggling to keep my balance, at first all I could think about was *not falling over*. But haven't you noticed that whatever you focus on, you get more of?

The fact is, *we think in pictures*. I call them "pictures of reality" because they become like magnets and attract the very things we're focused on. As long as I saw myself falling flat on my face, that's pretty much what happened. Now you might think that's a bit farfetched, but read on and I'll explain more.

CHAPTER 11

Focus, Focus, Focus

"Dancing faces you towards Heaven,
whichever direction you turn."

SWEETPEA TYLER, Author

H AVE YOU EVER LOOKED AT your life and wondered
why it doesn't *always* match what you *really* want?
Consider the possibility that what you say (or think) you want,
and what you spend your time focusing on, may not always be
the same thing. At least that's what Richard found out...

Richard's Story

When Richard was in his teens he lived on a cul-de-sac of about a dozen houses at the end of a fairly busy street in a small town in Northern England. One night, he decided to flex his boundaries and stay out way past his curfew.

It was late, and the neighborhood was quiet as he stealthily made his way along the street and up the path to his front door. Suddenly, out of nowhere, there was an absolute cacophony with the sound of glass smashing. Instantly, lights snapped on, curtains swung open, and shouts could be heard in the street.

Apparently, under the stress of thinking about what would happen if he was caught coming home so late, Richard forgot about the empty glass milk bottles standing like soldiers guarding the entrance to the front door. Normally, in the morning they would be magically replaced with full bottles of rich, creamy milk.

Richard was so focused on his thoughts that he didn't notice the milk bottles...until he walked right into them and sent the whole bunch crashing down the stone steps, making enough noise to wake the whole neighborhood.

Richard received a stern reprimand from his mom, not just for being so late, but also for making such a commotion. But what he remembered most was when his sister asked him the next morning, "What happened?" All he could say was, "I don't know. I was trying so hard not *to make any noise. I didn't want to wake anybody up, especially my mom."*

The whole thing perplexed Richard, and he continued to think about it, until one day he figured it out. He had been so focused on what he didn't want, and that was exactly what he created.

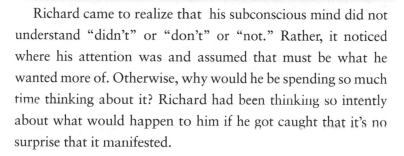

Richard came to realize that his subconscious mind did not understand "didn't" or "don't" or "not." Rather, it noticed where his attention was and assumed that must be what he wanted more of. Otherwise, why would he be spending so much time thinking about it? Richard had been thinking so intently about what would happen to him if he got caught that it's no surprise that it manifested.

Imagine that the Universe loves you, supports you, and wants you to have it all. But its only way of knowing what you want is to look at what you spend your time thinking about—what you *see* in your mind's eye. It then gives you even more of that! Even though Richard vividly recalls that he didn't want to wake his mom up, what he saw in his mind's eye was exactly that. And it came to pass. So Remember...

Whatever you focus on, you get more of!

While this may sound a bit farfetched, it is a simple phenomenon of nature. Noted educators Wheatley and Kellner-Rogers said, "Attraction is an organizing force of the universe,"[18] all the way from particles that are attracted to other particles to form atoms, to swirling gases that form stars, planets, and even solar systems.

A form of this universal law that dancers know a lot about is gravity. We don't have to know how it works or even believe in it to feel its effects.

So consider the possibility that whatever you focus on you get more of…

Why Are We So Focused on the Negative?

So why, then, do we often focus on what we *don't* want?

Just to clarify, there is nothing wrong with getting clear on what you don't want, especially when it comes to leading a more purposeful, engaged, enthusiastic life. But sometimes we can get stuck there. Remember I mentioned earlier that your brain has a built-in bias toward a negative fascination? Just think about the last meeting you attended at work. Was the focus primarily on all the wonderful things taking place? I didn't think so.

We have a natural bias toward a negative fascination because it is how our brains are wired. And this is a good thing!

Back in the days when we were hunters and gatherers, we always had to be on the alert for anything that might threaten our survival. According to Drs. Rick Hanson and Richard Mendius, because our ancestors were prey as well as predators, they were constantly looking over their shoulders, ready to run or attack depending on the situation. The ones who survived paid a lot of attention to *every potential threat*. As a result, they said, our brains were actually programmed to give higher priority to negative experiences over positive ones.[19]

There was an interesting study done at Vanderbilt University. Computer screens were divided into quadrants, and random faces that were either fearful, neutral, or happy appeared on the screen. The study participants had to hit a button as soon as they saw a face appear. Consistently, they were able to detect faces that had fearful expressions faster than neutral or happy ones, all because our brains give higher priority to negative experiences.[20]

Think about it...A person will tell twenty people about a bad experience at a restaurant but only tell one person about a good experience. Relationship expert John Gottman said that it takes five positive interactions in any relationship to counteract every negative one.[21]

This bias that our brains have could also explain why we are drawn to gossip and to watching reality TV. And do you notice that when something tragic happens in the world, we find ourselves glued to the news? That's because by default our brains are constantly on the lookout for what is wrong. It's just like Farmer Jim and the dog that walked on water. Let me explain.

There was a hunter who had been given a special dog that could walk on water. The trouble was nobody believed him, nor would they take the time to come and see for themselves. Finally, one day the hunter convinced old Farmer Jim, who was out working in his field, to take a walk with him down to the lake.

When they got there the hunter picked up a stick and threw it way out into the water. Sure enough the dog walked on the water, fetched the stick, and walked back. The hunter looked at the old farmer who seemed totally oblivious to what had just happened. The hunter thought that maybe the old farmer did not see well, so he threw the stick again. Once again, the dog walked on the water, fetched the stick, and brought it back.

Still there was no reaction at all from the farmer. So the hunter asked, "Did you notice anything special about my dog?" The elderly farmer thought about it for a moment or two, and then replied, "Now that you mention it, the stupid mutt can't swim!"

We laugh, but our brains are a bit like Farmer Jim's. By default they are constantly scanning for what's wrong. Then we wonder why we get so stressed.

The good news is that *we can change that*. And I'll tell you how.

The Amazing Brain

Until recently, scientists believed that your brain was "fixed" after early childhood. In other words, whatever you've got is what you are stuck with for life. But now we know that far from being fixed, your brain has amazing capabilities of changing its very structure.

For example, take Michelle. I was introduced to her in Norman Doidge's book, *The Brain that Changes Itself*.[22] Michelle is in her 30s and lives in Falls Church, Virginia. Like many of us, she loves good conversation, reading, and watching movies. Although Michelle has a few disabilities, she has a job, and in many ways her life is rather ordinary.

What is not ordinary about Michelle is that she only has half a brain. She's missing the entire left hemisphere because it never developed when she was in the womb. It was previously thought that different sections of the brain were allocated different functions, and if part of the brain was damaged, the corresponding function would be permanently lost. Not so! Not only can the brain grow new cells, but Michelle's right hemisphere rewired itself to take over the functions that her left hemisphere would normally control.

The implications are profound. But what does that mean to you? If your actions and thoughts can actually change the physical structure of your brain, which in turn influences how you think and feel, that means you have a lot more control over your mental and emotional states than was ever thought possible.

For example, every time you worry or awfulize, it's as if you just hit an internal panic button, and your body will prepare itself for fight or flight.

Have you ever noticed that when you even think about that meeting you are dreading on Monday morning, or that call you keep putting off, or the difficult client or boss that you have to work with that your heart begins beating faster, your palms start sweating, and your mouth goes dry like cotton? Adrenaline is flooding your system and you feel anxious *just thinking about it!*

Every time you worry or focus on negative consequences you add another layer of stress to your system. Soon you may not recognize how much stress you are carrying, and unchecked automatic responses will keep cycling through your body. Numerous research studies have identified that specific physical responses to negative emotions and unresolved stress can deplete us of energy and vitality.

In an ideal world you would realize that thinking about something that has not actually happened is a false alarm. Then your brain would send a message to your body, which would quickly relax back to normal. But with our busy lifestyles and the constant stream of noises, interruptions, and stressors (both real and imagined), our bodies have forgotten what it means to really relax.

To make matters worse, what we now know about the brain is that over time, if you keep hitting the panic button, it will actually learn to be stressed. Then it will start hitting the panic button for you, *even when there is nothing to panic about.*

But the opposite is also true. If your brain has learned to be stressed, there are things you can do to rewire your brain so you can experience more joy, enthusiasm, and satisfaction in life, even during challenging situations.

What if happiness was not something you were born with or solely the result of past or present circumstances? What if happiness was simply the result of your habitual thoughts and actions…and what if you could train your brain so you could be a happier, more enthusiastic person, no matter what challenges you had to face?

What if you could improve things once thought only to deteriorate or at best stay the same? I'm talking about your memory, your ability to focus, and even your I.Q. Wow! Yes, you really do have a lot more control than you probably realized. So how do you begin?

A good place to start is to notice when you are focusing on the negative, because that is a huge source of stress and we often don't realize we are doing it. Besides, it is hard to live with Full Wattage if you are always awfulizing.

Think about the negative message that is your biggest saboteur. Think about the one thing you tell yourself that *might actually hold you back* or that has held you back in the past.

Take a moment now and write down the one thing that stands out for you as your strongest negative self talk. For instance, you might tell yourself, "I am not qualified," "I am over-qualified," "I am not good enough," "I am a terrible money manager," "I am too old," "I am too young." Get the idea?

__ My most undermining negative self-talk is: (Pick *one* thing.)

_____

_____

_____

_____

_____

_____

The next time you catch yourself focusing on the negative, all you have to do is shift your fascination to the positive.

Shifting Gears

Shifting your thoughts from negative to positive sure *sounds easy.* I know from experience that it's usually easier said than done, because it goes against that basic survival instinct we talked about earlier. But maybe it doesn't always have to be so hard.

My husband, Francis, was going home to visit his family. He was on the plane that was going to take him from Baltimore to Minneapolis, and it was ready for takeoff. Francis was settling in for the flight when he noticed the woman sitting next to him looked ashen and was sweating profusely. He asked her, "Are you okay?"

"No," she said, "I'm terrified of flying." Then she added, "Actually it's not the flying. I don't really mind that at all. But the takeoff and landing scare me to death."

Then she noticed Francis was reading a book called *Energy Medicine*. She asked, "Are you into all that stuff?"

He replied, "Yes, I'm a health care practitioner."

"Well, can you help me?" she asked.

Francis turned to face her as best he could and asked, "May I take a look at your hand?" A little apprehensive, she agreed and held it out to him. He took her hand in his, turned it palm facing up, and said, "Wow, do you notice how this line goes all the way across your palm?"

As he spoke he traced the line on her hand with his finger. He continued, "But this line is very short and branches off here, and here. And look at this line. Do you see how deep it is? Mmmmmmm…," he said momentarily lost in thought.

Finally, not able to hold it in any longer the woman asked, "So, tell me…What does it mean?"

Francis looked up at her and said, "I have no idea. I'm not a palm reader. But look…" he said, pointing out the window.

She looked out the window and saw the clouds go by. She hadn't even noticed that the plane had taken off.

The mind can really only focus on one thing at a time. Sometimes it *is* simply a matter of changing your mind because you DO have the power to control where your attention goes.

The funny thing was, when it came time for the plane to land the woman tapped Francis on the shoulder and asked, "Can you do that thing again with my hand?"

When you find yourself overwhelmed, awfulizing, or simply worrying, here is a simple two-step process you can use.

The first step is to stop and take a deep breath. Try it with me right now. Take a nice slow inhale through your nose and let it out through your mouth. As you exhale, imagine you are cooling a bowl of hot soup. And again, take a nice *slow* inhale, really feeling the air as it comes in...and relax on the exhale. Ahhhhh! Isn't that better?

The second step is to ask yourself one of the most powerful questions of all. It is so simple but we often overlook it. Are you ready for it? The question is...

What do you want?

Yes, it's that simple. How *would* you like the situation to turn out? And even more important, how would *you* like to be? We often spend so much time worrying and focusing on what we don't want that it does not always occur to us to think about what we *do* want. Here is a powerful clarifying exercise for you.

Four Wants Exercise (Courtesy of Coach Shawn Moore)[23]

Ask yourself the following question four times out loud, each time emphasizing a different word. Listen and pay attention to how your body and emotions react as you go through this. Don't stop at the first answer you get. Allow yourself to go deeper to the truth of what you *really* want.

- **What** do you want?
- What **do** you want?
- What do **you** want?
- What do you **want**?

Don't forget to jot down your insights in your journal. This exercise can help you achieve greater clarity regarding your underlying beliefs about what you want.

Focus Your Attention

Remember earlier in the chapter when I asked you to write down your most undermining negative self-talk statement? To remind yourself, turn back to page 163 now and review what you wrote. Then come back here.

Now, imagine the most expansive, opposite thinking statement you can think of—the bigger and more outrageous the better. The only restriction is that is has to begin with the words, I AM. Write it here:

___I AM _____

_____

_____

_____

When you read your negative statement and then your positive one, it may feel a bit like a ping pong match. "I am not good enough: I AM perfect in every moment. I am not good enough…" That's normal, because we now know that by default your brain has always given priority to the negative things you have heard others say about you or you have told yourself.

Therefore, your positive I AM statement might be a little weak. So what do you do? You give it attention. Remember, *whatever you focus on, you get more of.*

Be ready for this to feel awkward as you become practiced in your new thought pattern. You are going to be altering an old habit and it's common to feel resistance. Being prepared for that resistance will give you a leg up.

So focus on your "I AM" statement. Use the power of repetition to change your negative affirmation into a positive one.

Realize that I'm not talking about affirmations the way people traditionally do them. The next chapter will tell you why.

CHAPTER 12

Learning to Dance in the Rain

"Life is not about waiting for the storm to pass...it's about learning how to dance in the rain."

VIVIAN GREENE, Author, Entrepreneur, and Passionate Dancer

THE YEAR WAS 1983. I was a struggling dance student and I was broke. But I had a great idea. I had heard about the power of affirmations and positive thinking, so I went to the dollar store and bought a bunch of fake million dollar bills. I stuck them all over the ceiling above my bed so I would see them first thing in the morning and last thing at night. I also put sticky notes all over my bathroom mirror, on the fridge, and all around my desk that said, "I am wealthy beyond imagination. All the money I need comes to me easily and in abundance."

Everything was wonderful...until my car broke down and needed $870 worth of repairs. At that moment, I lost my positive attitude and reverted to a scarcity mentality. All it took was one unexpected bill to challenge my newfound prosperity consciousness, and my positivity went out the window.

Does this mean that positive thinking doesn't work? Of course not. It's just that at the time, my new, fragile prosperity thoughts could not withstand the power *I was giving* to the negative thoughts.

Of course, I was making that choice. I was overwhelming my thoughts of abundance with fear and scarcity thinking. Even though I said I wanted to be wealthy, I was still constantly worrying about money and not having enough of it. So what was I *really* focused on? What did I keep reverting to? Lack! I discovered firsthand that what you say you want and *what you actually focus your attention on* are not always the same thing!

What Do You REALLY Want?

When it came to being wealthy, I wanted to believe I could create wealth. I hoped it could be true, and I tried to convince myself that it was true. But I did not buy it *at all!* I did not have faith that the Universe was indeed an abundant Universe. Nor did I feel deep down that I deserved or had the ability to manifest wealth. Despite my best intentions I continued to focus on how little I had.

And for a while, I stayed broke!

The Universe did not look at what I wrote on those sticky notes nor what I told myself 20 to 20,000 times a day. Instead, the Universe looked at what I *based my actions on.* It looked at what I was *calling real* by my thoughts, words, and deeds... then it gave me even more of that! But this didn't just happen to me. There are countless examples of people who fall into this trap. For instance…

- Think of the person who wants to be wealthy but saves the broken toaster for years…just in case he is able to fix it someday.

- Or how about the woman who keeps a wardrobe full of clothes that no longer fit her? Even if she ever did fit into them again some day, they'd be out of style. But she won't let them go.

- Then there's the guy who hoards every little thing because "you never know when you might need them."

In all these instances, the message being sent to the Universe is clear: "The Universe is *not* abundant, so you better hang on to what you have." Wow! Yes, it's subtle, but now you can probably see how this works.

CASE STUDY

Jonathon's Story

Jonathon was a workshop participant who wanted to make some lifestyle changes. Due to a combination of unfortunate circumstances and poor money management skills, he found himself with considerable credit card debt.

Despite his best intentions and a "debt reduction plan," he was having a hard time paying down his bills, which only created even more stress in his life.

I am not a financial advisor; however, I noticed that all Jonathon talked about, and all he seemed to focus on, was debt.

When I suggested to Jonathon that he open a savings account he thought I was nuts! And from a financial stand-point it did not make sense to put money in a low interest savings account when he was paying such high interest on his credit card debt. From a psychological perspective, however, it made perfect sense.

Jonathon started small. Each month when he paid his bills, he put a few dollars into his savings account. Watching it slowly grow was exciting for him and gave him hope.

We also changed the name of his "debt reduction plan" to his "financial abundance plan." Taking these few sim-ple steps shifted Jonathon's focus from debt to prosperity, from lack to abundance.

Of course, he still had to stick to a plan to pay off the debt he had accumulated, and he had to learn better money management skills. But his shift in focus made all the difference.

Jonathon shows that rather than focusing your energy on what you *don't* want, when you focus instead on what you *do* want, amazing things can happen! Where can you shift the fo-cus to abundance in *your* life?

What's Your Focus?

In his book, *Instructions to the Cook: A Zen Master's Lessons in Living a Life That Matters*, Bernhard Glassman writes that it was the Zen cook's duty to make the best meal possible using whatever ingredients he had, especially when feeling overstretched. Instead of focusing on all the ingredients he *would like* to have but didn't, the Zen cook started out by assessing everything he *did* have.[24]

We can all learn a lot from the Zen cook!

It's natural to think that the quality of our life would be so much better if we had the budget to include *everything* we could imagine. Yet I'm sure you've heard the phrase, "Necessity is the mother of invention." Even the renowned choreographer Twyla Tharp went so far as to say, "Whom the gods wish to destroy, they give unlimited resources."[25] I guess it's all a matter of attitude. In short, whatever you focus on, you get more of—whether it is lack or plenty.

So the next time things don't go the way you had planned and the floor starts rocking, take note: Are you focusing on negative consequences? If so, what would it take to let go of these things and put your attention instead on what you *do* want?

In what areas of life do *you* tend to get most stuck focusing on negative consequences? One of my clients is very successful in every area of her life, except when it comes to finding a life partner. Every date always ends with her telling herself, "I told you so; it *never* works out."

She is so attached to her beliefs that she won't find a life partner that she sabotages any chance of successfully finding someone. Her perfect partner could be staring her in the face and she would not even notice. Her pattern of focusing on negative consequences is stopping her from living a rich and full life shared with someone she loves.

How about you?

___The three specific areas in which I most tend to get stuck focusing on negative consequences are:

1. _____

   _____

2. _____

   _____

3. _____

   _____

When you read the "I AM" statement that you wrote on page 166, do you think that somewhere it could actually be *true* about who you are? Could it be true but just *not fully manifested yet*? Now that's food for thought.

What if your "I AM" statement is true about who you are in your natural state, but stress and life have interfered with that? When you think about it, all of the things we do to reduce stress are just things to take away the extraneous layers and the "noise" we have added, and to bring us back to our dynamic, energetic, creative, true self—back to our CORE.

When you say your "I AM" statement, say it from the place where it is true about you. In fact, stand up, put your hand over your heart, and *declare* your statement out loud to the Universe.

Go on, I dare you! If you are in a public place and can't do that, then speak the words internally loud and clear. Try it now!

Didn't that feel *powerful?* From now on, whenever you find yourself needing a boost, stand and declare your "I AM" statement to the world. Remember, whatever you focus on, you get more of.

When something comes along in life that rocks your boat and that does not match your vision, don't make a big deal of it. Do not let it throw you overboard like I did with the auto mechanic's bill! Just tell yourself it's an anomaly, and as soon as possible, get back to focusing on what you want.

Better yet, ask yourself how you can use the challenging situation to catapult you even closer toward your vision.

On the SS Uganda, I learned that we do not have to be the victim of external circumstances. Instead, we can use them as catalysts to move us forward. When I decided to integrate the movement of the rocking boat into my routine, it made my dance better!

This brings us to a myth I would like to dispel. I've often heard it said that once you get clear on what you want it will manifest effortlessly. The truth is, everything in the way of it manifesting is first likely to come up in your face, especially your own limiting beliefs. Then you end up with one foot on the gas pedal and one foot on the brake.

If you ever find yourself in that situation, here is a simple process you can use to reveal and then eliminate the limiting beliefs that might be getting in your way.

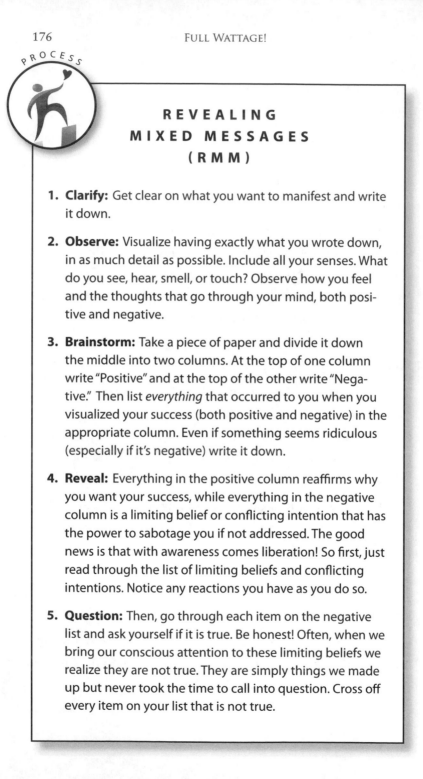

PROCESS

REVEALING MIXED MESSAGES (RMM)

1. **Clarify:** Get clear on what you want to manifest and write it down.

2. **Observe:** Visualize having exactly what you wrote down, in as much detail as possible. Include all your senses. What do you see, hear, smell, or touch? Observe how you feel and the thoughts that go through your mind, both positive and negative.

3. **Brainstorm:** Take a piece of paper and divide it down the middle into two columns. At the top of one column write "Positive" and at the top of the other write "Negative." Then list *everything* that occurred to you when you visualized your success (both positive and negative) in the appropriate column. Even if something seems ridiculous (especially if it's negative) write it down.

4. **Reveal:** Everything in the positive column reaffirms why you want your success, while everything in the negative column is a limiting belief or conflicting intention that has the power to sabotage you if not addressed. The good news is that with awareness comes liberation! So first, just read through the list of limiting beliefs and conflicting intentions. Notice any reactions you have as you do so.

5. **Question:** Then, go through each item on the negative list and ask yourself if it is true. Be honest! Often, when we bring our conscious attention to these limiting beliefs we realize they are not true. They are simply things we made up but never took the time to call into question. Cross off every item on your list that is not true.

6. **Formulate:** Sometimes, the beliefs and negative thoughts holding us back are based in truths. Still, there are often things we can do to reduce their impact on us.

   Look at each limiting belief still on your list that you think is true. Then, go through them one by one (if you have more than one) and ask yourself the following question: *"What could I do to reduce or eliminate the impact this challenge has on me?"*

   Write down any ideas that occur to you. (This is a great part of the process to do with a friend or a coach to guide you.)

7. **Plan:** Based on the ideas you generated in step six, create a simple plan that will help you deal with the real issues you are facing. Having this in place will deflate the beliefs that were holding you back and allow you to move forward. If you need further help with this, I recommend working with a coach or an accountability partner—someone who will help you stay on track.

My coaching client, Jessica, had a limiting belief holding her back. But it turned out that her belief was not even based in truth…

CASE STUDY

Jessica's Story

Jessica wanted to leave her job as a nurse practitioner and start her own clothing company. It was a dream she had nurtured for years, and she was taking steps toward manifesting it. But each time she got close to taking the big leap she sabotaged her efforts.

When we did the RMM process together, we saw that Jessica's mother had been a nurse and was delighted that her daughter had chosen to follow in her footsteps. Jessica thought her mother would be disappointed in her decision to leave nursing. Her desire to not disappoint her mother was keeping Jessica stuck.

However, when Jessica had a conversation with her mother, she learned that her mother was thrilled that she was following her dreams. In fact, her mother supported her decision 100 percent. The limiting belief that had been holding Jessica back was all in her own mind!

Carolyn, on the other hand, had a conflicting intention as a result of a real challenge she was facing in her business. Here's how she resolved it...

CASE STUDY

Carolyn's Story

Carolyn came to me for coaching because she needed more clients in her tax preparation business, yet she kept sabotaging her efforts to attract them.

When we did the RMM process we saw that Carolyn had a huge conflicting intention that she was not consciously aware of. Although she said she wanted more clients, she was already feeling overwhelmed with the demands of her current clients, as well as the needs of her family.

When she thought of having more clients, she thought of the extra work it would entail. So she unconsciously sabotaged her efforts. However, she knew that in order to reach her goals, her business had to grow.

Once I helped Carolyn become aware of why she was sabotaging herself, we were able to put a plan in place to help her feel less overwhelmed at work.

As a solo professional and CPA, Carolyn was offering bookkeeping for her clients as well as tax preparation. After going through the RMM process, she realized she did not have to do all the work herself.

Carolyn began by hiring a neighbor part-time who had excellent bookkeeping skills. That freed her up to focus on her clients' tax preparation needs, thus maximizing her skills and expertise. As she was doing more of the work she enjoyed, she was able to work at a higher energy level and got much more done.

Carolyn is no longer stressed out and trying to do everything herself. She now has one full-time and one part-time employee, has moved into a larger (and much nicer) office space, and works fewer hours.

As an added benefit, her obvious pleasure and confidence in her work has directly contributed to her attracting more clients. Carolyn's business is growing in leaps and bounds.

If you ever find yourself stuck and unable to move forward, like Carolyn or Jessica, give the RMM process a try. What it reveals may surprise you.

Always Move Forward

Have you ever had a limiting belief or thought pattern that you were sure you had let go of, only to have it return at a later time...and with a vengeance?

At times like this it's easy to think you have regressed—that you are going backwards. But consider the possibility that these patterns of thought are multi-faceted. Sometimes they show up in our lives again because a deeper layer is ready to be released. And that's a good thing! It's as though the time is right for you to deal with it.

In these moments, resist the urge to "beat yourself up" for being "back in that place again," especially when you thought you were over it! Instead of viewing it like a circle and you are back in the same place, imagine that it is more like a spiral and you have simply come around again, but on a higher level. If you take a good look you will notice that you are NOT in the same place—your perspective *is* different.

It is important that you acknowledge the progress you have made. Seeing your progress gives hope, encourages you to move forward, and nurtures your enthusiasm.

When these obstacles come up (which they inevitably will) repeat the RMM process to address these limiting beliefs so you can get back to focusing on the success you are striving to attain.

In fact, imagine that obstacles are the Universe's way of giving you a chance to take a stand for what you want. It's a way of asking, "Are you sure? Are you *really* sure this is what you want?" Every time you say YES and bring your focus back to what you *do* want, you reinforce your new reality and weaken the old one.

Remember, the obstacles that show up are life's gift to support you in bringing what you want closer to manifestation.

CHAPTER 13

Doing the Happy Dance

*"We're fools whether we dance or not,
so we might as well dance."*

JAPANESE PROVERB

IN CHAPTER 11 WE EXPLORED how your brain has a natural bias to focus on the negative, and I mentioned that there are many things you can do to change that. We already discussed the first strategy, which is to become aware of the tendency to awfulize and to consciously shift that. Remember, with awareness comes liberation!

Another way to reprogram your brain is to make a big deal when something goes really well. Hold it in your mind's eye. Really take in the experience. Hang onto it. Tell people about it. Celebrate it!

When something goes really well for me or my husband, we link arms and do the happy dance. For us, this is a sweet and memorable way to celebrate, and it gives us a moment to really claim the joy of success.

In Chapter 7 we discussed the power of celebrating your successes. What additional celebration rituals can you create? What would be fun and meaningful for you?

___To reinforce the positive and celebrate, I will:

1. _____

2. _____

3. _____

Besides, wouldn't *you* prefer to be around someone who celebrates the good things happening in their life rather than someone who is always complaining?

Anxiety Be Gone!

Do you ever wake up in the middle of the night and feel anxious for no apparent reason? Your brain starts scanning, scanning, scanning—looking for something to blame it on. Then it decides on something (a rather arbitrary process, I must admit) and pounces on it. That's when you start obsessing about it until there's *no way* you are going back to sleep.

Not sleeping well is a big source of stress in many people's lives. It's difficult to live with Full Wattage when you are sleep deprived and exhausted. So here is something you can do any time you feel anxious, but it is particularly powerful when you are trying to fall asleep. It will also help you sleep more soundly, which will increase your energy and enthusiasm during the day.

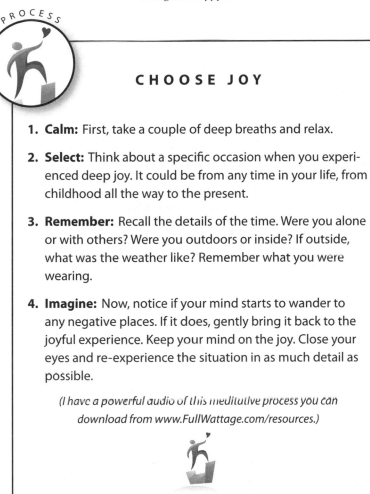

CHOOSE JOY

1. **Calm:** First, take a couple of deep breaths and relax.

2. **Select:** Think about a specific occasion when you experienced deep joy. It could be from any time in your life, from childhood all the way to the present.

3. **Remember:** Recall the details of the time. Were you alone or with others? Were you outdoors or inside? If outside, what was the weather like? Remember what you were wearing.

4. **Imagine:** Now, notice if your mind starts to wander to any negative places. If it does, gently bring it back to the joyful experience. Keep your mind on the joy. Close your eyes and re-experience the situation in as much detail as possible.

(I have a powerful audio of this meditative process you can download from www.FullWattage.com/resources.)

Did you do it? How do you feel now? Every time I do this process with a roomful of people, afterwards there is such a feeling of peace and calm in the room. How about you? Do you feel calmer and more peaceful from doing this process?

What science now demonstrates is that when you re-experience (or even imagine) a joyful or happy occasion, your brain rewires itself by *changing its neural structure*. Even if you only did this exercise for a few minutes a day, the impact on how you think and feel would be profound.

Remember, *whatever you focus on you get more of.*

What if you took a few moments each day to recall the times in your life when you felt the most purposeful? Or a specific time when you fully engaged your natural strengths and expressed your gifts to the world? Or the special occasions you treasure and value the most? Or what if you simply imagined living a totally meaningful, enthusiastic life, filled with wonder and joy? Wow!

The Joy Factor

I do not believe that joy is just an emotion or a feeling. To me, joy is a state of being. I'd even go so far as to say that joy is our natural state—the essence of who we are. That is why when you connect to your CORE, you experience joy.

Often, when we are not experiencing joy we think something is missing in our lives, like the perfect job, more money, a kinder boss, the latest gadget, our soul mate, etc. We then go off in search of that missing element. But have you noticed that the more you search "out there," the more disconnected you feel?

When we are not experiencing joy in our lives, it's not because something is missing; rather, *something is getting in the way.* Remember, joy is your natural state.

The renowned spiritual teacher, Torkom Saraydarian, said, "Joy is a state of beingness in which your consciousness is not conditioned by the environment or by the thoughts, emotions, and activities going on in your environment."[26]

Does that mean it's possible to experience joy no matter what the external circumstances? Even if your boss is stressing you out, you just lost your biggest customer, the kids are fighting *again*, the car has broken down and you're late for a job interview (a job that you *really* want)?

Torkom Saraydarian went on to say, "You have...joy, not because things and conditions are right or wrong, but because joy flows down from your core..."[27]

Your CORE is the essence of who you are. The more you connect to your CORE, the more you are connecting to your authentic self—to your reason for being, to your gifts and contribution to the world, to your values and what you truly believe in.

What if you *want* to spend more of your life connected to your CORE, but right now you are still feeling stressed out and are dancing as fast as you can just to get through the day?

I hear you! So let's address that next.

CHAPTER 14

Dancing As Fast As You Can?

"There are shortcuts to happiness,
and dancing is one of them."

VICKI BAUM, Author

W HILE YOU MIGHT LOVE THE idea of living a more purposeful, strength-based, values-driven life, what if you are dancing as fast as you can just to get through the day?

By now I hope you are beginning to see that when your CORE is at the foundation of your day-to-day life, you will naturally have plenty of energy, creativity, and enthusiasm. You will be more fully engaged and joyful. But when you are disconnected from your CORE, you may find yourself turning to other sources of energy, like adrenaline.

Adrenaline in and of itself is not a bad thing. In the short-term it helps our brains stay alert and our bodies active so we can get stuff done. But over time, relying purely on adrenaline as our energy source makes us *more tired* and even *more stressed out*. And it can make you sick. In that state, it is impossible to be balanced, fulfilled, and live with Full Wattage.

We may even become so depleted and burned out that we come to depend on that accelerated adrenaline rush. In fact, you might be an adrenaline junkie. How you can tell? Answer a few questions:

1. Do you feel that you do your best work when under pressure, especially when you have a deadline to meet?

2. How often do you get annoyed by people who drive exactly the speed limit, or even worse, under it?

3. Do you tend to feel an "inner rush" or impatience much of the time?

4. How often do you run on the late side or get somewhere "just in time" because you don't want to waste time sitting around if you get there early?

5. Do you ever find yourself getting caught up in dramas or arguments just because it energizes you?

6. Have you ever had a hard time winding down and switching off? Or relaxing? Even when you are on a vacation?

The more questions you answered "yes" to, the higher your possibility for being an adrenaline junkie. If you suspect you might be an adrenaline junkie and you want a more detailed quiz to find out, you can take the free self-test on the resource page of my website at www.fullwattage.com/resources.

Break the Habit

Allow me to share with you some practical activities that will not only reduce stress in your life and help break the adrenaline habit, but many of them will also help you to reconnect with your CORE. This list is by no means all-inclusive. These are simply some strategies that have worked for me and my clients.

Physical Exercise

Without a doubt, some form of physical exercise is a great way to break the stress cycle. Exercise pumps up your endorphins (feel-good hormones) and decreases your stress hormones. It also reduces chronic muscle tension, helps you sleep better, and decreases anxiety.

Exercise is also a natural way to increase your energy level, alertness, and concentration. But that's just the beginning.

In Chapter 11 we talked about the new breakthroughs in brain science and how our brain can actually learn to become stressed. In addition to simply increasing blood flow, and hence oxygen to the brain, we now know that physical activity *actually helps create new brain cells* or neurons, and helps them connect better with other nerve cells. In other words, exercise is a powerful way to help you rewire your brain.

But not all exercise is created equally. When it comes to rewiring the brain, the best form of physical exercise is one that also involves focus and concentration. So activities like tennis, soccer, and the myriad of exercise classes at your local gym are good. However, learning a *new* physical activity is an even better way to take care of your stress levels for the short-term, as well as rewiring your brain for long-term health.

Dance

Dance is also a powerful stress reducer, especially learning new moves, which can be both physically and mentally challenging. In fact, many schools in the United Kingdom now teach ballroom and Latin dance because of the positive effect it has on the children's learning abilities and behavior.

And if you guys think that manly men don't dance, think again. According to *Psychologies* magazine, Dr. Peter Lovett, a psychologist specializing in performance at the University of Hertfordshire in England, recently examined how women respond to men's dance moves at nightclubs.

He discovered that shufflers (those who simply shuffle from foot to foot) were rated lowest in terms of masculinity and attractiveness, while those who incorporated the occasional unexpected movement were "eye-catching and appeared more in control."[28] So who says manly men don't dance!

Yoga and Pilates

Yoga and Pilates are also powerful ways to decrease stress and increase energy, feelings of self-worth, and overall enthusiasm for life. Both of these practices incorporate controlled breathing, increased blood flow, hand-eye coordination, and complete body-mind awareness.

Massage

One of my favorite ways to interrupt the stress cycle is to get a relaxing, therapeutic massage. It reminds the body of what it feels like to let go. And when the body lets go, the mind does too. A rested mind is more resilient and operates with greater clarity.

When asked how she deals with the stress of running a successful business and raising a family, Kristina Bouweiri, CEO of Reston Limousine (one of the top 10 largest shuttle bus fleets in the U.S.), said, "I get a massage every week, and for that one hour someone else is taking care of me. And that rejuvenates me for the whole week."

Stretch

If you are sitting for extended periods of time, particularly at a computer, a few stretches can revitalize and energize you.

Baths

Take a long bath, especially with fragrant aromatherapy oils.

Walk

Take a walk in the fresh air (in sunshine is even better).

Be in Nature

Any time you spend in nature can be calming, healing, and uplifting. It is one of the best ways to renew yourself. So take an occasional trip to the ocean, or the mountains, or to your favorite lake or river. Perhaps you prefer the coolness of the forest, or the fragrance of the desert. And when was the last time you stared at the stars on a crystal clear night? If you can't actually get out into nature, at least surround yourself with flowers and plants indoors.

Listen to Music

Listening to beautiful, calming, energizing, or uplifting music is powerful. In fact, studies show that listening to Mozart in the background can help with concentration. This is called "The Mozart Effect."[29] Try it sometime.

As a Business Specialist at Southwest Research Institute, Rosemary Ryan spends much of her day in business development and administrative activities, not to mention her two-and-a-half-hour daily commute in Washington D.C. traffic!

At the end of the day (and especially when she feels anxious or worried) she plays one of her favorite pieces of music, the Pavane in F-sharp minor, Op. 50, by the French composer Gabriel Fauré. As it plays, Rosemary feels relaxation washing over her (though she says she loves that piece of music so much that she plays it when she feels good too!).

Create Music

Playing (or learning to play) a musical instrument can also be rejuvenating.

Sylvia Lagerquist, CPA, has a lifelong love of playing the piano and the flute. In her work as President and Owner of Haines & Lagerquist, CPAs, LLC, she serves as an outsourced CFO for small businesses. That requires creative thinking and excellent problem solving skills.

In addition to helping her rest and relax, Sylvia says that playing music stimulates her creative thinking and increases her efficiency and effectiveness in the office. She also shares her passion for music with clients and business acquaintances by holding concerts in her home.

Fan the Fire

Watching controlled firelight is relaxing. I often light a candle before beginning a creative project. You can also sit by a fire and just stare into the flames.

Turn to Your Friends

Get together with friends and just have fun.

Cynthia de Lorenzi, CEO of the dynamic and unconventional business networking group Success in the City (Washington D.C.), said," The most valuable assets I have are my friendships."

She's not alone in thinking that. A recent Harvard Study showed that having strong social bonds not only makes us feel better, but can also promote brain health as we get older.[30]

Additionally, Rebecca G. Adams, a professor of sociology at the University of North Carolina, Greensboro, said, "Friendship has a bigger impact on our psychological well-being than family relationships."[31]

Which of your friends can you most rely on for comfort and nurturing? What about for inspiration and energy? Who do you turn to for acknowledgement? Or for advice or clarification about something? Who is your cosmic cheerleader? And who will hold your feet to the flames and tell it like it is, no matter what?

Friends are not always one-size-fits-all. Sometimes you need to get specific about the type of support you desire as well as who may be best to provide it. So who is on your dance card?

Meditate

Another way to relax and still an overactive mind is to practice some form of meditation, or even just do some deep breathing with awareness. Here is a specific breathing exercise you can use to either calm and focus you, or uplift and energize you.

Breathing Meditation

1. **Connect:** Put one hand on your belly and one hand one your solar plexus. Your solar plexus is right in the middle of the upper half of the trunk of the torso, where the rib cage comes together at the stomach level in front of the diaphragm.

2. **Slow Down:** Take a nice long inhale through your nose, and exhale through your mouth. Imagine you are cooling a hot bowl of soup.

3. **Expand and Soften:** As you inhale, feel the solar plexus and belly gently expand into your hands, and as you exhale feel them soften and relax.

4. **Lengthen:** With each breath make the inhale and exhale a little longer.

5. **Energize:** If you are feeling tired or sluggish and want to energize your body and brain, *focus on the inhale* and make it twice as long as the exhale.

6. **Calm:** If, on the other hand, you want to calm and relax your body and mind, *focus on the exhale* and make it twice as long as the inhale.

Breathing with awareness is such a powerful way to interrupt the stress response in your physical body. So stop right now and take a few deep, focused breaths. Ahhhhh!

Renew Yourself

I just shared with you a number of ways to break the stress and adrenaline habit, and at the same time rejuvenate yourself. So take a few moments now to think about the ways *you* like to revitalize and renew yourself. What helps put you in a positive state of body and mind?

This will be very personal, because what works for one person may not work for another. Also, different activities may work better for you in different situations depending on what you need at the time. Therefore, pay attention to what your body, mind, and spirit are calling out for.

For example, if you are feeling hyper and anxious, lighting a candle may not do it, but some physical activity might. *Then,* you might benefit from sitting quietly with a beautiful candle.

Being in tune with yourself and your needs will help you make better choices as to how to best manage your personal energy.

___ **My favorite ways to de-stress and re-energize are:**

1. _____

2. _____

3. _____

4. _____

5. _____

For additional ideas on ways to break the stress cycle, go to www.fullwattage.com/resources.

The next question is, "How can you integrate more of these activities into your day-to-day life so you can experience more energy, joy, and enthusiasm?" That's coming up, so read on!

CHAPTER 15

Dance to Your Own Rhythm

"Everything in the universe has rhythm. Everything dances."

MAYA ANGELOU, Poet, Educator, Actress

JEN WAS FEELING OVERWHELMED AND certainly lacking in the enthusiasm department. She had three children under the age of six, a demanding career, and a husband who had recently been promoted to a great job that required a considerable amount of travel. Jen wanted to support her husband in his exciting new position (which in the long-term would allow her family many more opportunities due to his increased salary), but she felt exhausted and her lights were on dim. She desperately wanted to get back to living with Full Wattage.

I encouraged Jen to make a list of the activities she enjoyed that energized and uplifted her. It took her a while to come up with a list, as it had been a long time since she had even thought of the activities she enjoyed. But once she got going, it became easier.

I also asked her to make a list of the activities that calmed and focused her.

The next step was for Jen to write down how long she would have to do each activity in order to feel energized or calm, depending on what she most needed at the time.

Jen had some activities on her list that only took a few minutes, like listening to a favorite upbeat song, and some that took longer, like soaking in a luxurious bath with aromatherapy oils. I also suggested that she include activities she could do at work, even right at her desk.

What would your lists look like?

Take a few moments now to think about the activities that energize or calm you. Next to each activity, write the amount of time needed for it to have the desired effect.

If thinking about doing any of these things makes you feel either silly or guilty, then you're on the right track.

Energizing Activities   **Time Needed**

_____   _____

_____   _____

_____   _____

_____   _____

_____   _____

_____   _____

_____   _____

Calming Activities	Time Needed

Keep your list where you can easily access it when you need it most. Then, the next time you need to pick your energy up, or calm yourself down, look at your list. Then choose an activity based on how much time you have available. Yes, it really is that simple.

I have a template of this list you can download and print at www.fullwattage.com/resources. Now there is no excuse not to have your list handy! Just being prepared to support yourself will make a noticeable difference in your life.

Give Yourself a Time Out

You *still* might think you don't have time to do the things on your list. But when you are stressed, taking a short time out to re-energize yourself and focus will help you to be more productive in the long run.

Let's say there is a part of your personal or work life that's exhausting. Maybe there is an activity you know you *have* to do for now, but it's not a strength of yours. Can you think of something specific?

___ Even though I know it is not a strength of mine, an activity or task I must still do (for now) is:

_____

Think about how you feel for the rest of the day every time you engage in that activity. I would imagine you don't feel too inspired. What if you scheduled the time to do something energizing right before and especially right after the draining activity to counterbalance the negative effects?

For example, have you ever had to meet with a very demanding or high maintenance relative, friend, client, or customer and it negatively affected your whole day? What if you were to schedule your time with them just before lunch, and as soon as you were done you went for a nice brisk walk...or played your favorite upbeat music...or took two minutes to stretch or dance. Whew! Do you think that might have an impact on the rest of your day?

I also suggested that Jen keep track of her energy levels throughout the day. I specifically asked her to notice the times of day when her mental focus was clearest, her physical energy was strongest, her creative energy was at its peak, and she felt the most productive. Then we helped her build her day around that.

Jen learned to save her more routine tasks, which required less mental energy, for the times of day when it was naturally lower. That way she could maximize the periods when her productivity and creativity were at their peak. No more being out of sync!

What about you? What is your natural rhythm? How could you build your day around that?

__I am most mentally alert between the hours of:

_____

I am most creative between the hours of:

_____

My physical energy is strongest between the hours of:

_____

I am the most productive between the hours of:

_____

My energy is at its lowest between the hours of:

_____

Is Multitasking Overrated?

One final thing: I have always prided myself on my ability to multitask, but now I'm thinking it's a bit overrated. It seems that the more my attention is divided, the more stress it creates.

Just this morning I was brushing my teeth with my electric toothbrush when I decided to walk into my adjacent home office to scan my emails. Just as I was doing that the phone rang. Without thinking, I took the electric toothbrush out my mouth (yes, it was still running) to answer the phone. Toothpaste sprayed everywhere! Having my attention on multiple things at once definitely added to my workload (though I did stop to laugh at myself first).

It may not be true for you (that multitasking creates more work), and it may not be true for me *all* the time. But from now on, when I find myself multitasking, I plan to stop and ask myself, "Would I get the job done faster, and with less stress, if I just did each task with full attention?"

What about you? If your energy was clearly focused, what do you think you might be able to create in your life?

Speaking of creativity, would it help if you had a little more? If so, that is next.

CHAPTER 16

Take Time to Play

"And those who were seen dancing were thought to be insane by those who could not hear the music."

FRIEDRICH WILHELM Nietzsche, Philosopher

WHEN YOU ARE STRESSED, HOW does that affect your creativity? If you are like most people, you may experience that initial adrenaline rush when under pressure. But the more stress goes up, creativity (as well as enthusiasm) generally goes down.

But remember the lesson I learned on the SS Uganda: By being fully aware and connected to my CORE I flowed with the situation and performed well, despite challenges. Realize that no matter what the situation, no matter how stuck you feel, you have a lot more control than you might think. You can choose to stay stuck, or you can be bold and do something about it.

Of course, putting into action all the ideas we already explored to reduce stress in your life will increase your creativity. It also helps if you can break out of your normal habits for a short period of time. One of the best ways to break out of your routine is to bring more playfulness and spontaneity into your life, especially into your work environment. You will find that some of your most creative flashes will come when you are having fun...if you allow yourself!

Ann McGee-Cooper in *Time Management for Unmanageable People* wrote, "...the more we work, the more tired we get, the less creative or open-minded we are, and the less we accomplish, so we get further behind and then we think we have no time for play."[32] Isn't that the truth!

Be Different!

When you need to inspire your creativity, here are some additional activities to help you get out of your normal groove and do something different.

Be a Kid Again

Think about some of the things you loved to do as a child. The more fun and wacky, the better! Did you ever build a fort with sofa cushions? Play outside in a hailstorm? Climb a tree? Allow a friend to blindfold you and guide you around? Swing on a rope? Whittle a stick?

What did you love to do? Is there a way you can incorporate any elements of those things into your workday?

Sue's Story

As a child, my client Sue used to love raking huge piles of leaves and jumping into them. So one day, when she was feeling particularly frustrated about a project at work, she went out to the local park at lunchtime, found a private spot, gathered a huge pile of leaves, and kicked and jumped around in them.

She admitted that at first, she was kicking up the leaves in anger and frustration. But after a few minutes she was laughing out loud. Sue went back to work feeling lighter and definitely in a better mood. Taking time to play increased her energy and released the tension she had been feeling. That, along with the laughter, gave her a fresh perspective, and she was able to view her project from a much more resourceful place.

Sue said the best laugh of all was when she got home that evening and her daughter asked her about the leaf stuck to the back of her jacket. Nobody had mentioned it all afternoon!

Don't underestimate the power of laughter. In fact, Dr. Lee S. Berk, a preventive care specialist and psychoneuroimmunology researcher at Loma Linda University's Schools of Allied Health and Medicine, and his colleagues have done numerous studies on laughter.

What they found was that repetitious "mirthful laughter," which they call Laughercise©, causes your body to respond in a way similar to moderate physical exercise. Dr Berk said that laughter enhances your mood, decreases stress hormones, enhances immune activity, lowers bad cholesterol and systolic blood pressure, and raises good cholesterol.[33] And that's no laughing matter!

Think about those days that you know are going to be tough on you and prepare for them, as preparation is powerful. Planning to take a break to add fun and playfulness to your day will actually re-energize you and get the creative juices flowing so you get more done in less time. And you'll be healthier too.

___ Some of the fun, playful, wacky things I loved to do as a child were:

1. _____

2. _____

3. _____

___ I could integrate elements of these things into my day by:

1. _____

2. _____

3. _____

Get Out and Get Inspired

Get out of your office or the physical space you spend the most time in. Take a trip to an art gallery, a park, or even the mall! You never know where inspiration will strike.

When I find myself really stuck or frustrated with something, my husband will often come into my home office and insist that I come with him. Then he hands me my motorcycle jacket and helmet, and off we go for a ride on our bike (called Wind Horse). I almost always resist at first because "there's work to be done." But once I get over that limiting perception I have a blast sitting on the back of our bike, feeling the wind on my face and watching the world go by. It just takes a few minutes and I am rejuvenated. In fact, I get some of my best ideas when we are out on Wind Horse.

When you go out to get inspired, carry a notepad or voice recorder with you. That way, when that next great creative idea or solution to a problem pops up, you will be ready.

Move

When you are feeling stuck, one of the easiest ways to get unstuck is to *get up and move*. One of my mentors, Gabrielle Roth, said, "Movement is medicine...a dynamic way to free the body, to express the heart, and to clear the mind."[34]

The next time you are feeling out-of-sorts, I invite you to put on your favorite upbeat music and dance around to it. Don't worry about feeling awkward. As the wonderful choreographer Twyla Tharp said, "Get over yourself!"[35]

In fact, you could even try it NOW. Go on, give it a whirl. Find your favorite dancing music and rock out! If you are in a public place (like at work) and it is *not* appropriate to be seen whirling and twirling, put on a headset for a few minutes, turn up the music, and *imagine* yourself dancing wildly. It's *almost* as good.

Did you do it? If so, how does your energy feel now versus before you got up and moved?

There is an amazing connection between physical movement and the brain. In fact, in *The Brain That Changes Itself*, Norman Doidge wrote, "Nothing speeds brain atrophy more than being immobilized in the same environment."[36] So you are probably not going to have your best creative ideas when you're sitting at your desk. Get up, dance around, go for a walk, just *move*.

We often associate things like memory loss with getting older. But what if it was simply the result of us becoming less active?

Focus

If you are working on a creative project at work or at home, sometimes you may need frequent breaks. But on other occasions, you will need to set aside chunks of time with no interruptions to really get the creative juices flowing. And, yes, that means no checking email or text messages, no status updates, and no answering the phone.

Jakob Neilson, Ph.D., a Usability Consultant, said that "...even a one minute interruption can easily cost a knowledge worker 10 to 15 minutes of lost productivity due to the time needed to reestablish mental context and reenter the flow state."[37]

Protect your focus by not allowing distractions to break your attention and get you off track.

How can you create boundaries where you'll be uninterrupted?

___I can create boundaries for uninterrupted time by:

1. _____

2. _____

3. _____

Remember, no matter what situation you are in, *you have a lot more control than you think.* Let go of the things you have no control over. Put your attention instead on all the things you can do to increase your energy, productivity, creativity... and enthusiasm!

When you do that, you will find it is even easier to connect to your CORE and live with Full Wattage!

CHAPTER 17

Dig Deep and Bend Like the Wind

"Dancing should look easy; like an optical illusion. It should seem effortless. When you do a difficult variation, the audience is aware that it is demanding and that you have the power and strength to do it. But in the end, when you take your bow, you should look as if you were saying, 'Oh, it was nothing. I could do it again.'"

BRUCE MARKS, Principal Dancer, American Ballet Theatre

O NE RECENT SUNDAY AFTERNOON I was working at my desk, when suddenly my computer screen went blank. The power had gone out. Seconds later there was a loud roaring noise.

I looked out the window of my home office and saw that every plant and bush was blowing sideways. All the branches on the trees were also streaming to the side. Even the trunks of the trees appeared to be bending in the wind.

Actually, not all of them were bending. There was one MASSIVE tree whose trunk did not appear to be moving at all.

I watched in fascination.

Then, before my eyes, the massive tree ever so slowly tipped over and toppled to the ground. It was surreal. Even though it was only a few feet away, it seemed to fall in complete silence. (I realized later that the noise of the wind had completely drowned out the sound of the tree hitting the ground.)

At that point I decided it may be a tornado and took refuge in the bathroom in the center of the house. Our home is surrounded by trees and I didn't know what else might come down.

Fortunately, the storm passed as quickly as it came. When all was still again I ventured outside to take a look. I saw branches and tree limbs *everywhere*. But that huge tree was the only one that was actually knocked over by the storm. Of all the trees in the area, it was one of the biggest. So why did it fall?

When I looked at the tree's base, I noticed there were few roots. For a tree that big, I was amazed. Although it looked like such a solid tree, it had no depth of foundation under it. The wind was easily able to knock it over.

How about you? Are your roots big and deep? Do you have a strong foundation?

If you have been following the suggestions in this book then you *will* have deep roots because you will be connected to your CORE—to the things in life that are most essential to you.

You will be well on the path to knowing your sense of purpose, your reason for being, a calling greater than yourself. You will have discovered your unique strengths, talents, and gifts, and you will know how to build your life around them.

You will have prioritized your values to give them the time and energy they deserve.

Throughout this book we have looked at how to build a strong foundation and deep roots so you will be able to weather any storm.

But there was one other thing I observed when watching the trees. During the storm, while all the other trees bent to various degrees, dancing in the wind, the tree that fell had remained upright and unbending.

It reminded me of the time I was struggling to keep my balance on the SS Uganda. At first I was resisting, unyielding, willing myself not to fall over. That did not work. But then I had a huge lesson: *It was only by digging deep and connecting to my CORE that I was able to yield and bend like the wind.*

In Chapter 2, I mentioned the often surprising fact that, as dancers, we spend most of our time off balance. That might not be apparent when your think about a ballet dancer effortlessly poised en pointe, hanging motionless, balanced for what seems like an eternity on the very tips of her toes.

The secret is…the ballerina is not static at all. It's an illusion. If you watched very closely you would see that she is in a constant state of fluid movement. Being connected to your CORE is a dynamic, not static, state of being. As such, a dancer can be connected to her CORE and yet be flexible, just like the trees in the wind. In fact, the more a dancer uses her CORE strength, the greater the risks she can take in her movements.

How Far Can You Bend?

Have you ever watched an inexperienced dancer move? Because they have not yet strengthened their CORE, they often stay within their comfort zone and are very predictable and boring to watch. But as they gain experience and develop their CORE strength, they become much more exciting and dynamic. They move out of their comfort zone and learn to "bend like the wind."

The same is true in life. Sometimes I work with clients who are feeling stuck. They have become "too balanced," stagnant, and bored. They're in a rut and don't know how to get out of it.

These are the clients who come to me and say, "I know I really have nothing to complain about. I love my husband and kids. I have a good job. There is nothing really *wrong*. It's just that I feel I am going through the motions of life. Something is missing, but I'm not sure what."

When I look in their eyes I can see they are not living with Full Wattage (or even close). It's time for them to dig deep and bend like the wind. It's time they leave behind their old routines and step up to new challenges—to live *their* life dance.

What about you?

We have explored in great depth what it means to dig deep and connect to your CORE. But are you also able to bend with the winds and storms in your life?

Bending with the wind means letting go of all the preconceived ideas, thoughts, and beliefs that are holding you back. It means not being attached to how things were in the past, but seeing things through fresh eyes as they are *now*. It means throwing out all the things that no longer serve you—letting go of the habits, self-talk, and old self-images that constrict you.

Human beings are not designed to be static. Life is in a constant state of flux. *You* are in a constant state of flux. The spirit of life is flowing through you. You are not the "you" that you were five years ago, or even five minutes ago. In *every moment* you have the opportunity to let go of all the baggage you are carrying and be *new.*

What would it take for you to reinvent yourself *today* as that person who is full of vitality and enthusiasm, and is living with Full Wattage?

What are you carrying that stops you from being *magnificent*? What keeps you living small? What are you ready to let go of?

___ In order to live with Full Wattage I am ready and willing to let go of:

1. _____

2. _____

3. _____

Being all you can be is a courageous journey. Since you've read this far, my hope is that you have no other choice—that you are committed to living with Full Wattage, no matter what!

Besides, why settle for anything less than being fully, dynamically, enthusiastically alive?

I admit, it won't always be easy. We are living in incredibly tumultuous times. Nothing is the same as it once was. The world economy is going through an upheaval. We are currently seeing unprecedented worldwide extreme weather and natural disasters. A wave of unrest is crossing the face of our planet as the repressed and previously silenced are demanding their voices be heard.

On top of that, the internet and social media are changing everything, from the way we do business to how we communicate and stay connected with our friends and family.

Let's face it, the boat IS rocking. When you resist it—even push against it—you will be as powerless as that huge tree. Every time I look out my office window there is a big space where it used to stand. It is a constant reminder to me that no matter how hectic life gets, each day I must connect to my CORE, dig my roots deep, and bend with the wind. What about you?

CHAPTER 18

Your CORE Brilliance

"While I dance I cannot judge, I cannot hate, I cannot separate
myself from life. I can only be joyful and whole.
That is why I dance."

HANS BOS, Patron of Dance

T HROUGHOUT THIS BOOK I HAVE asked you a lot
of questions; now it's time for one more. Given that we
are living in such unprecedented times, do you think it is just a
coincidence that you happen to be alive at this particular time
in our planet's history?

Consider for a moment that there is a specific reason for
your existence. Maybe you have a unique part to play—a part
that *nobody* could play but you.

Could it be that the longing you have felt in your heart to
live more fully is in response to this calling?

I do believe we each have a calling and a precise timing as to when we are called. The fact that you have read this far makes me wonder…Perhaps your time is *now*.

Live with Full Wattage!

So many people are living lives that are way too small, with their lights barely flickering at best. What if your contribution to humanity was to live your life with Full Wattage *now*, as a demonstration of what is possible and to spread that light wherever you go? What if you allowed your CORE brilliance to shine, even when life is hard?

You can do that; I know you can. You just have to remember to stay grounded in your authentic truth…in your CORE of:

- Your **Purpose** – Your calling, your reason for being.
- Your **Strengths** – The things you do best and that you love to do.
- Your **Values** – What truly matters most to *you*.

To remind you one last time…

C = **Clarify** your purpose, strengths, and values.

O = **Organize** your life around those key elements as much as possible.

R = **Release** the saboteurs that are holding you back.

E = **Enthusiasm**, energy, and en-JOY-ment will be yours.

As you continue on your journey to fully expressing all that you are and all that you came here to do and to be, remember this: If you ever find yourself feeling overwhelmed and under-rested…Or there is too much to do and not enough time…Or things don't go exactly the way you planned…then take a deep breath and get centered by connecting to your CORE, to what matters most *to you.*

You will do amazing things!

I have shared with you the secrets I learned on the SS Uganda as I tried to keep my balance in a raging North Sea storm. Those lessons have served me well ever since. I hope they serve you, too.

I know that if you apply them to your life, not only will you be able to keep your balance in challenging times, but you will also be filled with joy, enthusiasm, and passion, no matter how much the floor is rocking. And you *will* live life with Full Wattage!

> *"So be encouraged and dedicate yourself to your dream, and if your dream should come my way one day then we will dance upon the boards of life."*

BEN VEREEN, Dancer, Actor, Singer

Bibliography and References

1. *The Profitable Power of Purpose,* Ian Percy, Inspired Productions Press, LLC, 2004

2. *Riverdance a Journey,* directed by John McColgan , produced by Tyrone Productions 1995

3. *The Purpose Linked Organization: How Passionate Leaders Inspire Winning Teams and Great Results,* Alaina Love and Marc Cugnon, McGraw Hill, 2009

4. Martha Graham, quoted by biographer Agnes de Mille in *Martha: The Life and Work of Martha Graham, 1991*

5. *Now Discover Your Strengths*, Donald Clifton and Marcus Buckingham, Free Press, 2001

6. Gallup, Inc http://www.gallup.com/consulting/61/Strengths-Development.aspx Accessed 12/7/11

7. *Now Discover Your Strengths*, Donald Clifton and Marcus Buckingham, Free Press, 2001

8. Gallup, Inc http://www.gallup.com/consulting/61/Strengths-Development.aspx Accessed 12/7/11

9. *A Return To Love: Reflections on the Principles of A Course in Miracles*, Marianne Williamson, Harper Collins, 1992

10. *The Millionaire Messenger*, Brendon Burchard, Simon & Schuster, 2011

11. Ibid

12. Quoted by David Whyte at a live workshop in Annapolis, MD, 2009. Originally from his poem, *Sweet Darkness*

13. *The Carrot Principal*, Adrian Gostick and Chester Elton, Free Press, 2009

14. I have seen many versions of this process, but I was first exposed to it in Loral Langemeier's Big Table coaching program. This has been adapted from that process.

15. 2010 Survey conducted by the Conference Board Research Group (Authored by John M Gibbbons, Report # R-1459-09-RR). This was the lowest level of job satisfaction ever recorded in more than 22 years of studying the issue.

16. *She Works Hard For The Money* lyrics © Universal Music Publishing Group, 1983

17. "awfulize." *The Oxford Pocket Dictionary of Current English.* 2009. Encyclopedia.com. www.encyclopedia.com.

18. *A Simpler Way!* Margaret J. Wheatley, Myron Kellner-Rogers Berrett-Koehler Publishers, Inc., 1998

19. *Buddha's Brain,* Rick Hanson, Ph. D. with Richard Mendius, MD, New Harbinger Publications, 2009

20. E. Yang, D. Zald, and R. Blake, 2007 http://zaldlab.psy.vanderbilt.edu/Publications/assets/ey07emo.pdf

21. John Gottman, The Gottman Relationship Institute

22. *The Brain that Changes Itself*, Norman Doidge, M.D., Penguin Books, 2007

23. Shawn Moore is a personal coach and colleague www.BaronessBuilders.com

24. *Instructions to the Cook: A Zen Master's Lessons in Living a Life That Matters*, Bernhard Glassman and Rick Fields, Three Rivers Press, 1997

25. *The Creative Habit: Learn It and Use It for Life,* Twyla Tharp, Simon & Schuster, 2005

26. *Joy and Healing*, Torkom Saraydarian, T.S.G Publishing Foundation, Inc., 1987

27. Ibid

28. *Psychologies* magazine, Hearst Magazines UK, the National Magazine Company Ltd.

29. 1993 paper in *Nature* (vol 365, p 611) Rauscher, Shaw and Ky, "Music and Spatial Task Performance." Additional studies were done by Rauscher and Li Hong Hua (2004) Rideout in 1996, Wilson and Brown in 1997, Nantais and Schellenberg in 1999, and Martin and Sword in 2004.

30. *Effects of Social Integration on Preserving Memory Function in a Nationally Representative US Elderly Population*, Karen A. Ertel, M. Maria Glymour, Lisa F. Berkman, Harvard School of Public Health, American Journal of Public Health 2008

31. NY Times article "What Are Friend's For? A Longer Health" http://www.nytimes.com/2009/04/21/health/21well.html

32. *Time Management for Unmanageable People: The Guilt-Free Way to Organize, Energize, and Maximize Your Life*, Ann McGee-Cooper with Duane Trammell, Bantam Books, 1994

33. Federation of American Societies for Experimental Biology. "Body's response to repetitive laughter is similar to the effect of repetitive exercise, study finds." ScienceDaily, 26 Apr. 2010.
American Physiological Society. "Laughter Remains Good Medicine." ScienceDaily, 17 Apr. 2009.

34. *Sweat Your Prayers: Movement as a Spiritual Practice*, Gabrielle Roth, Tarcher Putnam, 1997

35. *The Creative Habit: Learn It and Use It for Life*, Twyla Tharp, Simon & Schuster, 2005

36. *The Brain that Changes Itself*, Norman Doidge, M.D., Penguin Books, 2007

37. Nielsen J (2003) IM, Not IP (Information Pollution). Queue, 76-75

About the Author

ORIGINALLY FROM SCOTLAND, LIZ FLETCHER BROWN was awarded a First Class Honors B.A. in Dance in the U.K. She then went on to fulfill a successful career as a dancer in New York City, Los Angeles, London and Tokyo. (One of her more unusual assignments resulted in her being featured as *the first full-sized dancing hologram at Madame Tussaud's Waxwork Museum in London* next to Marie Antoinette and Elvis Presley.)

Liz now enjoys a career as a keynote speaker, workshop facilitator, life coach and counselor. As a thought leader in the field of personal transformation, she specializes in high energy, motivational, and content-rich keynotes and workshops.

Liz brings to all of her work an infectious enthusiasm and a unique combination of engaging stories, practical ideas, and dance as a dramatic teaching metaphor, to enhance peoples' working and personal lives.

As an active member of the National Speakers Association, and a member of the Board of Directors of NSA Washington

D.C., Liz stays on top of current trends and innovations in the industry.

Liz received her coaching credentials from Success Unlimited Network™, one of the oldest coach training organizations in the U.S., and is a graduate of the School of Small Business Coaching. In addition, she is a certified trainer with Consulting Resource Group International, a global leader in personal and professional development solutions.

Liz is also a certified counselor and a member of the International Association of Applied Psychology and an Associate of the International Positive Psychology Association.

When she was 21, Liz moved from Scotland to New York City, to a country where she knew no one, to follow her dream of being a professional dancer. As a lifetime entrepreneur, this adventuring spirit continues to motivate her today.

Next Steps...

ARE YOU READY TO FULLY express and manifest your CORE brilliance in all areas of your life? Do you want to feel *alive* with a sense of passion and purpose? Is it *your time* to create a life worth celebrating and to live with Full Wattage?

Would you like support with that? Then you may want to consider CORE Brilliance Coaching.

Core Brilliance Coaching helps you connect to that place where you:

- tap into your own inner wisdom and answers.
- more rapidly and consistently produce the results you want in life, while increasing your overall well being.
- integrate your purpose, values and beliefs in all you do.
- fully express your natural strengths, gifts and talents.
- are clear, focused, self-assured and energized.

When you live from your CORE Brilliance you are filled with vitality, joy and enthusiasm, because you are living in alignment with who you truly are.

Who is CORE Brilliance Coaching for?

You may be feeling stuck or dissatisfied in one or more areas of your life. Perhaps you are going through a major transition, or would like to make significant changes in your life. Maybe you would like to explore a completely new direction.

You may have a business, or would like to start a business, and want it to be meaningful as well as profitable and fun. Or perhaps you are not really clear on what you want but you know this is NOT it!

If any of these apply to you, then CORE Brilliance Coaching may be a perfect fit.

I'd like to know more. What's next?

The next step is to contact us to schedule an "exploratory" session. You can do that at: coaching@fullwattage.com

From time to time Liz offers teleclasses, webinars, live workshops, and online group coaching programs. For more information, visit www.FullWattage.com

If you're ready to dance out of the wings and into the spotlight of your life...to get bigger about who you are...to step forth into your magnificence...to live with Full Wattage, then come and join us. You can find us at:

www.FullWattage.com
www.facebook.com/fullwattage
www.pinterest.com/lizfbrown

Have Liz Speak at Your Next Event

IN HER KEYNOTES AND WORKSHOPS, Liz will provide your audience with an entertaining and thought-provoking presentation, through her unique combination of engaging stories, practical tools, humor and dance.

Liz offers programs on: *Work and Life Balance, Purpose and Motivation, Self Esteem and Empowerment, Personal Excellence, Attitude and Performance.*

As a result of her work, people experience:

- a greater sense of self worth.
- a more positive outlook on what they can accomplish.
- a better understanding of themselves and others.
- a greater realization of the impact of the choices they make.
- more energy, enthusiasm, creativity and joy.

This leads to greater success and fulfillment, both personally and professionally.

Here are 5 more reasons to get Liz on your dance card for your next meeting or event:

1. **Memorable and Engaging Presentation Style**
   Liz's use of dance as a dramatic teaching metaphor, combined with her powerful stage presence developed over a lifetime of being a performance artist, makes the delivery of her message unique, engaging, and memorable.

2. **Experience**
   Liz has been helping her clients enhance the quality of their lives through her workshops and presentations since 1989. During that time she has helped thousands of people live with more purpose, more confidence, more focus, and have the right attitude for success, even in challenging times.

3. **Participants Love Her**
   Liz consistently receives excellent scores from participants on session feedback forms. For testimonials visit www.LizFletcherBrown.com

4. **A Joy to Work With**
   Liz knows what it's like to work with prima donnas (literally) and she isn't one. Enough said!

5. **Flexibility**
   Liz is flexible. Yes, she can kick her leg up to her nose, but that is not what we mean here. She wants to meet, maybe even exceed, your needs and can adapt and adjust when circumstances call for it. Just don't ask her to tap dance in pointe shoes!

For more information, and a listing of available programs visit **www.LizFletcherBrown.com**